QUINTILIAN INSTITUTE
1101 N. Highland St. #522
Arlington, Virginia 22201

COINTELPRO
THE FBI'S SECRET WAR ON POLITICAL FREEDOM

Edited by Cathy Perkus

Introduction by Noam Chomsky

Monad Press, New York

This book includes, in revised form, material from the following issues of
the *Militant:* March 28, April 4, April 11, April 18, April 25, May 9, May
16, May 30, June 13, July 4, July 11, and August 8, 1975. This material is
used by permission.

Information about the suit against government harassment by the
Socialist Workers party and the Young Socialist Alliance, and copies of
all Cointelpro files made public in connection with it, are available from
the Political Rights Defense Fund, Box 649 Cooper Station, New York,
N.Y. 10003. Telephone (212) 691-3270.

Files concerning Muhammad Kenyatta are available from the American
Civil Liberties Union, 22 East 40th Street, New York, N.Y. 10016.

Files concerning the Black Panther party are available from the
December 4 Committee, 53 West Jackson, Chicago, Ill. 60605. Telephone
(312) 341-9766.

A MONAD PRESS BOOK

Distributed by:
Pathfinder Press
410 West Street
New York, N.Y. 10014

Contents

Preface

"CO-INTEL-PRO" is FBI lingo for the bureau's illegal (and once top secret) "Counterintelligence Program." Cointelpro was designed to go beyond spying to the actual disruption of the political activities of American citizens—legal activities protected by the Bill of Rights.

What kind of people and organizations become targets of the FBI? What do they stand for? How does FBI harassment affect them and how have they been able to fight back?

The story of Cointelpro is told best in the FBI's own words, in language never intended for the eyes of the American people. The chapters that follow provide documented case studies of Cointelpro in action against Black activists, antiwar leaders, and socialists. The files come straight from the FBI. The accompanying essays are based on research and interviews with the victims by Nelson Blackstock, Nancy Cole, and Baxter Smith; this material was originally prepared for the socialist newsweekly the *Militant*.

The FBI is not a willing source of information about any of its clandestine operations, especially the disruption programs it waged in secret for at least fifteen years. Files have to be pried out of its vaults by lawsuit. And even then the documents are heavily censored by the bureau before they are released.

The first successful suit of this kind won disclosure of some key Cointelpro files in December 1973 and March 1974. It was a Freedom of Information Act suit by NBC-TV reporter Carl Stern. The files he got were those initiating several Cointelpro operations. Noam Chomsky, in his introduction, describes these.

Most of what is now known about the day-to-day disruption

tactics of Cointelpro has been made public as a result of the landmark civil liberties suit by the Socialist Workers party and the Young Socialist Alliance. An order by Federal Judge Thomas P. Griesa produced FBI disclosures in March, June, and October 1975 totalling 4,000 pages, a thousand of them from Cointelpro files. A sampling of these records makes up the core of this book. The letters and memos chronicle ten years of the FBI's work to derail the civil rights and antiwar movements and drive a legal political party out of existence.

The socialists' suit aims to expose and curb the FBI's attacks on constitutional rights. It seeks $27 million in damages and a permanent injunction outlawing harassment of all those who dissent from official policy. Prominent constitutional attorney Leonard Boudin and his associate Herbert Jordan took the case to court July 18, 1973.

The Cointelpro papers have been widely distributed by the Political Rights Defense Fund, the nonpartisan civil liberties group that is financing and supporting the socialists' case.

The story of Cointelpro is slowly emerging. In the process, proof accumulates that Cointelpro harassment of political activists continues to this day—despite assurances by top government officials that the programs known as Cointelpro were formally ended in April 1971.

CATHY PERKUS
Political Rights
Defense Fund

Introduction

Beginning in the fall of 1971, some curious events took place in Detroit, Michigan. In late October, lists of supporters, contributors, and subscribers to the party newspaper were stolen from the campaign headquarters of the Michigan Socialist Workers party. A few months later, the home of a Socialist Workers party organizer was robbed. Valuables were ignored, but membership lists and internal party bulletins were stolen. The burglaries remain unsolved.

If we ask who might be interested in obtaining the stolen material, a plausible hypothesis suggests itself. The natural hypothesis gains support from the fact that persons whose names appeared on the stolen lists were then contacted and harassed by FBI agents, and a personal letter of resignation from the party, apparently stolen from the headquarters, was transmitted by the FBI to the Civil Service Commission. Information that has since been obtained about FBI activities, including burglaries over many years, lends further substantiation to the conclusion that the FBI was engaged in one of its multifarious endeavors to undermine and disrupt activities that fall beyond the narrow bounds of the established political consensus.

The Detroit events recall another incident which, with its aftermath, became the major news story of 1974. But it would be misleading to compare the Detroit burglaries to the Watergate caper. If, indeed, the FBI was responsible, as seems most likely, then the Detroit burglaries are a far more serious matter. If the conclusion is correct, then in Detroit it was the political police of the national government which, in their official function, were engaged in disrupting the "sanctity of the democratic process,"

9

not merely a gang of bunglers working "outside the system."

The ousting of Richard Nixon for his misdeeds was described in the nation's press as "a stunning vindication of our constitutional system."[1] The Detroit example, and others far more serious to which I return, suggest a rather different reaction. There is a fundamental distinction between Watergate and Detroit. In the case of the events surrounding Watergate, the victims were men of power who are expected to share in the ruling of society and the formation of ideology. In Detroit the victims were outsiders, fair game for political repression of a sort that is quite normal. Thus it is true, in a sense, that the punishment of Nixon and his cohorts was a vindication of our system, as this system actually operates in practice. The Nixon gang had broken the rules, directing against the political center a minor variant of the techniques of repression that are commonly applied against radical dissent. If the basic work of repression continues, after Nixon, without appreciable comment or concern, then this too will show that the system is functioning, quite in accord with ample historical precedent.

Assuming FBI involvement, the Detroit incident is nevertheless minor in comparison with other facts exposed during the past several years. From December 1973, the government was compelled through several civil suits to release documentary evidence concerning its various campaigns to undermine and disrupt legal activities directed to social change or simply protest against state policy, through the decade of the 1960s. In comparison with these revelations, the whole Watergate affair was a tea party. The documents and depositions made public during this period, and revelations by disaffected government agents, lay bare a systematic and extensive program of terror, disruption, intimidation, and instigation of violence, initiated under the most liberal Democratic administrations and carried further under Nixon. The Department of Justice, in its apologetic and fragmentary review, asserts that the "counterintelligence program" (Cointelpro) operations "were apparently not reported to any of the Attorneys General in office during the periods in which they were implemented," apart from "certain aspects of the Bureau's efforts to penetrate and disrupt the Communist Party USA and White Hate Groups."[2] Assuming this assertion to be true, we may still observe that government officials who had even a passing familiarity with FBI practices in the past had a definite responsibility to determine how the bureau was acting, under their authority.

A review of these programs demonstrates the relative insignificance of the charges raised against Nixon and his associates, specifically, the charges presented in the Congressional Articles of Impeachment.[3] Further insight into the state of American society can be derived by the following simple exercise: compare the attention focused on the Watergate episodes by the mass media, including the liberal press and journals of opinion, with the reaction to the exposures, during exactly the same period, of the FBI programs. This exercise will demonstrate that until the dust had settled over Watergate, there was virtually no mention of the government programs of violence and disruption or comment concerning them, and even after the Watergate affair was successfully concluded, there has been only occasional discussion. The *New Republic,* which at that time could fairly be considered the semiofficial organ of American liberalism, was unconcerned by these exposures, though hardly an issue passed without a denunciation of Nixon for his crimes, trivial by comparison. With a few honorable exceptions (specifically, the *Nation*), the same was true more generally. The Watergate affair thus reveals quite clearly the subservience of the media to power and official ideology. The example is a particularly telling one, given that the media are so commonly hailed for their courage and independence during this period.

The lesson of Watergate is simple. American liberalism and the corporate media will defend themselves against attack. But their spirited acts of self-defense are not to be construed as a commitment to civil liberties or democratic principle, despite noble and self-serving rhetoric. Quite the contrary. They demonstrate a commitment to the principle that power must not be threatened or injured. The narrow "elites" that control the economy, political life, and the system of conventional doctrine must be immune to the means of harassment that are restricted, in the normal course of events, to those who raise a serious challenge to ruling ideology or state policy or established privilege. An "enemies list" that includes major corporate leaders, media figures, and government intellectuals is an obscenity that is seen as shaking the foundations of the republic. The involvement of the national political police in the assassination of Black Panther leaders, however, barely deserves comment in the national press, including the liberal press and journals, with rare exceptions.

The Cointelpro operations of the 1960s were modeled on the successful programs of earlier years undertaken to disrupt the

American Communist party. Though details are unknown, these programs were no secret, and were generally regarded as legitimate. The programs directed against the Communist party continued through the 1960s, with such interesting innovations as Operation Hoodwink from 1966 through mid-1968, designed to incite organized crime against the Communist party through documents fabricated by the FBI, evidently in the hope that criminal elements would carry on the work of repression and disruption in their own manner, by means that may be left to the imagination.[4]

From the evidence now available, it appears that the first FBI disruption program (apart from the CP) was launched in August 1960 against groups advocating independence for Puerto Rico. In October 1961, the "SWP Disruption Program" was put into operation against the Socialist Workers party. The grounds offered, in a secret FBI memorandum, were the following: the party had been "openly espousing its line on a local and national basis through running candidates for public office and strongly directing and/or supporting such causes as Castro's Cuba and integration problems . . . in the South." The SWP Disruption Program, put into operation during the Kennedy administration, reveals very clearly the FBI's understanding of its function: to block legal political activity that departs from orthodoxy, to disrupt opposition to state policy, to undermine the civil rights movement.

These basic commitments were pursued in subsequent years. For example, the Phoenix office of the FBI noted in a memorandum of October 1, 1968, that Professor Morris Starsky of Arizona State University, "by his actions, has continued to spotlight himself as a target for counterintelligence action." These "actions" consisted of the following crimes against the state: "He and his wife were both named as presidential electors by and for the Socialist Workers Party when the SWP in August, 1968, gained a place on the ballot in Arizona. In addition they have signed themselves as treasurer and secretary respectively of the Arizona SWP." Nothing further is alleged, though an earlier memorandum (May 31, 1968) identifies Starsky as one of those who have provided "inspiration and leadership" for "New Left organizations and activities in the Phoenix metropolitan area," so that he is one of "the most logical targets for potential counterintelligence action." The memorandum suggests that "reliable and cooperative contacts in the mass media" should be helpful in this particular program of "Disruption of the New Left." The documents in the Starsky case also indicate that prior to the targeting of Starsky on October 1, the FBI had somehow influenced the Board of Regents that controls the university to "find cause to separate Professor STARSKY from the public payroll" on trumped-up charges (memorandum of July 1, 1968).

Similarly, the comprehensive program to "expose, disrupt, and otherwise neutralize the activities of the various New Left organizations, their leadership and adherents," secretly put into operation in May 1968, was motivated by the fact that New Left activists "urge revolution," are responsible for unspecified "violence and disruption," "call for the defeat of the United States in Vietnam," and "continually and falsely allege police brutality and do not hesitate to utilize unlawful acts to further their so-called causes." They have even "on many occasions viciously and scurrilously attacked the Director and the Bureau in an attempt to hamper our investigation of it and to drive us off the college campuses," where, naturally, the state's political police should be free to operate with impunity. The latter offense was particularly grave since, as is now known, FBI provocateurs were engaged in extensive efforts throughout the country to instigate campus violence, disrupt student groups, eliminate radical faculty, and the like, and FBI agents were, for example, engaged in such actions as stealing documents from campus groups and burglarizing the offices of professors supporting them.[5]

The commitment of the FBI to undermine the civil rights movement, despite an elaborate pretense to the contrary (and even some actions as government policy vacillated on the issue), will come as no surprise to people with first-hand experience in the South in the early 1960s. As late as summer 1965, FBI observers refused to act within their legal authority to protect civil rights demonstrators who were being savagely beaten by police and thrown into stockades (some, who tried to find sanctuary on federal property, were thrown from the steps of the federal building in Jackson, Mississippi, by federal marshals). These efforts continued in later years, as, for example, when the FBI, under Cointelpro, succeeded in driving a Black minister from the Jackson Human Rights Project in early 1969, causing him to leave the South altogether, by sending him a "spurious, threatening letter" and encouraging school and church officials to file complaints against him on the basis of charges which (according to his ACLU lawyer) were fabricated by the bureau and "derogatory" information provided by the bureau.[6]

Predictably, the most serious of the FBI disruption programs were those directed against "Black Nationalists." These programs, also initiated under liberal Democratic administrations, had as their purpose "to expose, disrupt, misdirect, discredit, or otherwise neutralize the activities of black nationalist, hate-type organizations and groupings, their leadership, spokesmen, membership, and supporters, and to counter their propensity for violence and civil disorder." Agents were instructed "to inspire action in instances where circumstances warrant." Specifically, they were to undertake actions to discredit these groups both within "the responsible Negro community" and to "Negro radicals," and also "to the white community, both the responsible community and to 'liberals' who have vestiges of sympathy for militant black nationalists simply because they are Negroes. . . ."

Several model actions were proposed to agents, who were instructed "to take an enthusiastic and imaginative approach to this new counterintelligence endeavor," including an action apparently directed against the Student Nonviolent Coordinating Committee (SNCC) in 1967, in which local police, alerted by the FBI, arrested leaders "on every possible charge until they could no longer make bail" so that they "spent most of the summer in jail and no violence traceable to [censored] took place." In this case too, agents were directed to use "established local news media contacts" and other "sources available to the Seat of Government" to "disrupt or neutralize" these organizations and to "ridicule and discredit" them. In the light of these documents, one cannot fail to recall the elaborate subsequent campaign, in this case abetted by several liberal intellectuals and "democratic socialists," to ridicule and discredit individuals who attempted to raise funds for the Black Panthers during the period when they were being subjected to extensive police and judicial attack.

During these years, FBI provocateurs repeatedly urged and initiated violent acts, including forceful disruption of meetings and demonstrations on and off university campuses, attacks on police, bombings, and so on. Meanwhile, government agencies financed, helped organize, and supplied arms to right-wing terrorist groups that carried out fire-bombings, burglaries, and shootings, all with the knowledge of the government agencies responsible[7]—in most cases the FBI, although one right-wing terrorist in Chicago claims that his group was financed and directed in part by the CIA.[8] One FBI provocateur resigned when he was asked to arrange the bombing of a bridge in such a way that the person who placed the booby-trapped bomb would be killed. This was in Seattle, where it was revealed that FBI infiltrators had been engaged in a campaign of arson, terrorism, and bombings of university and civic buildings, and where the FBI arranged a robbery, entrapping a young Black man who was paid $75 for the job and killed in a police ambush.[9] In another case, an undercover operative who had formed and headed a pro–Communist Chinese organization "at the direction of the bureau" reports further that at the Miami Republican convention he incited "people to turn over one of the buses and then told them that if they really wanted to blow the bus up, to stick a rag in the gas tank and light it" (they were unable to overturn the vehicle). The same ex-operative contends that Cointelpro-type operations, allegedly suspended in April 1971, were in fact continuing as late as mid-1974, when he left the bureau's employ.[10]

Many details are now available concerning the extensive campaign of terror and disruption waged by the government during these years, in part through right-wing paramilitary groups organized and financed by the national government but primarily through the much more effective means of infiltration and provocation. In particular, much of the violence on campus can be attributed to government provocateurs. To cite a few examples, the Alabama branch of the ACLU argued in court that in May 1970 an FBI agent "committed arson and other violence that police used as a reason for declaring that university students were unlawfully assembled"[11]—150 students were arrested. The court ruled that the agent's role was irrelevant unless the defense could establish that he was instructed to commit the violent acts, but this was impossible, according to defense counsel, since the FBI and police thwarted his efforts to locate the agent who had admitted the acts to him. William Frapolly, who surfaced as a government informer in the Chicago Eight conspiracy trial, an active member of student and off-campus peace groups in Chicago, "during an antiwar rally at his college, . . . grabbed the microphone from the college president and wrestled him off the stage" and "worked out a scheme for wrecking the toilets in the college dorms . . . as an act of antiwar protest."[12] Many such cases have been exposed throughout the country.

Perhaps the most shocking story concerns the assassination of Fred Hampton and Mark Clark by Chicago police directed by the state's attorney's office in December 1969, in a predawn raid on a Chicago apartment. Hampton, one of the most promising leaders of the Black Panther party—particularly dangerous because of his opposition to violent acts or rhetoric and his success in community organizing—was killed in bed, perhaps drugged. Depositions in a civil suit in Chicago reveal that the chief of Panther security and Hampton's personal bodyguard, William O'Neal, was an FBI infiltrator. O'Neal gave his FBI "contacting agent," Roy Mitchell, a detailed floor plan of the apartment, which Mitchell turned over to the state's attorney's office shortly before the attack, along with "information"—of dubious veracity—that there were two illegal shotguns in the apartment. For his services, O'Neal was paid over $10,000 from January 1969 through July 1970, according to Mitchell's affidavit.

The availability of the floor plan presumably explains why "all the police gunfire went to the inside corners of the apartment, rather than toward the entrances," and undermines still further the pretense by the police that the police barrage was caused by confusion in unfamiliar surroundings that led them to believe, falsely, that they were being fired upon by the Panthers inside.[13]

Agent Mitchell was named by the *Chicago Tribune* as head of the Chicago Cointelpro directed against the Black Panthers and other Black groups. Whether or not this is true, there is now substantial evidence of direct FBI involvement in this gestapo-style political assassination.

O'Neal, incidentally, continued to report to Mitchell after the raid. He was taking part in meetings with the Hampton family and discussions between lawyers and clients, one of many such examples of violation of the lawyer-client relation. To cite another, which did receive considerable publicity, the chief security officer of the American Indian Movement, also a paid FBI informer, "was the only person, other than defendants and lawyers, with regular access to the room in which defense strategy was planned." So valuable were his services during this period that his cash payment from the bureau was raised from $900 to $1,100 a month. "The Government, in a sworn affidavit at the trial, had appeared to contend that it had no informer in the defense ranks." The informer, who came to believe that AIM was, in his words, a "legal, social organization that wasn't doing anything wrong," reports also that he helped lead an armed take-over of a state office building in Iowa, among other tasks performed for the FBI.[14]

A top secret *Special Report* for the president in June 1970[15] gives some insight into the motivation for the actions undertaken by the government to destroy the Black Panther party. The report describes the party as "the most active and dangerous black extremist group in the United States." Its "hard-core members" were estimated at about 800, but "a recent poll indicates that approximately 25 per cent of the black population has a great respect for the BPP, including 43 per cent of blacks under 21 years of age." On the basis of such estimates of the potential of the party, the repressive agencies of the state proceeded against it to ensure that it did not succeed in organizing as a substantial social or political force. We may add that in this case, government repression proved quite successful.

The same *Special Report* develops the broader motivation for the FBI operations. The intelligence analysis explains that "the movement of rebellious youth known as the 'New Left,' involving and influencing a substantial number of college students, is having a serious impact on contemporary society with a potential for serious domestic strife." The New Left has "revolutionary aims" and an "identification with Marxism-Leninism." It has attempted "to infiltrate and radicalize labor," and after failing "to subvert and control the mass media" has established "a large network of underground publications which serve the dual purpose of an internal communication network and an external propaganda organ." Its leaders have "openly stated their sympathy with the international communist revolutionary movements in South Vietnam and Cuba; and have directed others into activities which support these movements." "Although New Left groups have been responsible for widespread damage to ROTC facilities, for the halting of some weapons-related research, and for the increasing dissent within the military services, the major threat to the internal security of the United States is that directed against the civilian sector of our society."

In summary, during the decade of the 1960s and for a period of unknown duration since (perhaps still continuing), the FBI extended its earlier clandestine operations against the Communist party, committing its resources to undermining the Puerto Rico independence movement, the Socialist Workers party, the civil rights movement, Black nationalist movements, the Ku Klux

Klan, segments of the peace movement, the student movement, and the "New Left" in general. The overall allocation of FBI resources during this period is of course unknown. One relevant bit of evidence is provided by the "Media files," stolen from the Media, Pennsylvania, office of the FBI in March 1971 by a group calling itself "the Citizens' Commission to Investigate the FBI," and widely distributed through left and peace movement channels. According to its analysis of the documents in this FBI office, 1 percent were devoted to organized crime, mostly gambling; 30 percent were "manuals, routine forms, and similar procedural matter"; 40 percent were devoted to political surveillance and the like, including two cases involving right-wing groups, ten concerning immigrants, and over 200 on left or liberal groups. Another 14 percent of the documents concerned draft resistance and "leaving the military without government permission." The remainder concerned bank robberies, murder, rape, and interstate theft.[16] Whether these figures are typical or not we cannot know, in the case of a secret organization like the FBI. It is clear, however, that the commitment of the FBI to undermine and destroy popular movements that departed from political orthodoxy was extensive, and was apparently proportional to the strength and promise of such movements—as one would expect in the case of the secret police organization of any state, though it is doubtful that there is anything comparable to this record among the Western industrial democracies.

The effectiveness of the state disruption programs is not easy to evaluate. Surely it was not slight. Black leaders estimate the significance of the programs as substantial. Dr. James Turner of Cornell University, president of the African Heritage Studies Association, assesses these programs as having "serious long-term consequences for black Americans," in that they "had created in blacks a sense of depression and hopelessness."[17] He states that "the F.B.I. set out to break the momentum developed in black communities in the late fifties and early sixties"; "we needed to put together organizational mechanisms to deliver services," but instead, "our ability to influence things that happen to us internally and externally was killed." He concludes that "the lack of confidence and paranoia stimulated among black people by these actions" were just beginning to fade. Conceivably, the long-term impact may be salutary: "We realize that we can't depend on symbolism and on inspired leadership and we are beginning to build solidly based organizations."

SAC, New York   October 12, 1961

Director, FBI

SOCIALIST WORKERS PARTY
INTERNAL SECURITY - SWP
DISRUPTION PROGRAM

       The Socialist Workers Party (SWP) has, over
the past several years, been openly espousing its line
on a local and national basis through running candidates
for public office and strongly directing and/or supporting
such causes as Castro's Cuba and integration problems
arising in the South. The SWP has also been in frequent
contact with international Trotskyite groups stopping
short of open and direct contact with these groups. The
youth group of the SWP has also been operating on this
basis in connection with SWP policies.

       Offices receiving copies of this letter are
participating in the Bureau's Communist Party, USA,
Counterintelligence Program. It is felt that a disruption
program along similar lines could be initiated against the
SWP on a very selective basis. One of the purposes of this
program would be to alert the public to the fact that the
SWP is not just another socialist group but follows the
revolutionary principles of Marx, Lenin and Engels as
interpreted by Leon Trotsky.

       It is pointed out, however, that this program
is not intended to be a "crash" program. Only carefully
thought-out operations with the widest possible effect
and benefit to the nation should be submitted. It may
be desirable to expand the program after the effects have
been evaluated

       Each office is, therefore, requested to carefully
evaluate such a program and submit their views to the Bureau
regarding initiating a SWP disruption program on a limited
basis.

*1961 FBI letter initiating the Socialist Workers Party
Disruption Program. It cites the party's electoral activities,
defense of Cuba, and support for the civil rights movement,
not any alleged violent or illegal actions.*

The faculty and a great majority of the students at the school were very distressed and upset with the foolish and extremist activities of JACKSON and his associates, as was evidenced by the forming of the Defense Committee. Additionally, they felt that the programs of the BPP and its representatives and associates was a program of nihilism.

III. PROPOSED COUNTERINTELLIGENCE MEASURE

It is proposed that the following letter be typewritten on commercial paper and forwarded to DONALD JACKSON at his Hillcrest Street residence at Tougaloo, Mississippi, bearing Tougaloo, Mississippi, postmark:

> "Tougaloo College
> Tougaloo, Mississippi
>
> Date

"Muhammed Kenyatta---

"The deplorable activities and conduct of you and your Black Panther brothers at the recently completed Black Spring Weekend have shocked the Tougaloo College community into realizing the basic errors in the intimidation methods and nihilistic doctrines which you promote. Your immature actions of discharging firearms near the campus on Saturday afternoon, April 11, further alienated you and you 'outsiders' from the spirit and tone in which all desired the BSU to take. Your recent involvement in various criminal activities in and near Tougaloo College as well as your irresponsibility in paying your school bills while at Tougaloo College further exemplify the inappropriateness of you, of all people, in any manner acting as a representative of blacks in Mississippi or anywhere for that matter. Your conduct and demeanor is representative of traits and habits we in our quest are trying to rise above.

Pages 20 and 21: Among the fifty pages of Muhammad Kenyatta's Cointelpro file is this letter warning the civil rights leader to leave Mississippi or face measures "which

"Accordingly, it has been determined by solidity representative elements of the Tougaloo College Student Body that you are directed to remain away from this campus until such time as your conduct and general demeanor reach the desired level. This directive also applies to your bringing any of your unruly and undisciplined associates to the campus."

"Should you feel that this is a hollow directive and not heed our diplomatic and well thought out warning we shall consider contacting local authorities regarding some of your activities or take other measures available to us which would have a more direct effect and which would not be as cordial as this note.

"Tougaloo College Defense Committ:

IV. OBJECTIVE

It is hoped that this letter, if approved and forwarded to JACKSON, will give him the impression that he has been discredited at the Tougaloo College campus and is no longer welcomed there. It could discourage him from inviting out of state extremists to visit him and while here to speak at Tougaloo College. It may possibly also cause him to decide to leave Mississippi and return to his original home in Pennsylvania.

V. RECOMMENDATION

would have a more direct effect." The threat is attributed to Tougaloo students.

nationalist activity, and interested in counterintelligence,
to coordinate this program. This Agent will be responsible
for the periodic progress letters being requested, but each
Agent working this type of case should participate in the
formulation of counterintelligence operations.

GOALS

For maximum effectiveness of the Counterintelligence
Program, and to prevent wasted effort, long-range goals are
being set.

1. Prevent the coalition of militant black
nationalist groups. In unity there is strength; a truism
that is no less valid for all its triteness. An effective
coalition of black nationalist groups might be the first
step toward a real "Mau Mau" in America, the beginning of
a true black revolution.

2. Prevent the rise of a "messiah" who could
unify, and electrify, the militant black nationalist movement.
████████ might have been such a "messiah;" he is the martyr
of the movement today. ███████████████████████████████████
████████████ all aspire to this position. ████████████████
████████ is less of a threat because of his age. ███████████
be a very real contender for this position should he abandon
his supposed "obedience" to "white, liberal doctrines"
(nonviolence) and embrace black nationalism. ██████████████
has the necessary charisma to be a real threat in this way.

3. Prevent violence on the part of black
nationalist groups. This is of primary importance, and is,
of course, a goal of our investigative activity; it should
also be a goal of the Counterintelligence Program. Through
counterintelligence it should be possible to pinpoint potential
troublemakers and neutralize them before they exercise their
potential for violence.

4. Prevent militant black nationalist groups and
leaders from gaining respectability, by discrediting them
to three separate segments of the community. The goal of
discrediting black nationalists must be handled tactically
in three ways. You must discredit these groups and
individuals to, first, the responsible Negro community.
Second, they must be discredited to the white community,

*Pages 22 and 23: Communication from J. Edgar Hoover,
dated March 4, 1968, putting into effect the Cointelpro—
Black Nationalist-Hate Groups. It raises questions about
FBI complicity in the murders of Malcolm X and Martin
Luther King, Jr. Under goal 2, their names fit perfectly in*

both the responsible community and to "liberals" who have vestiges of sympathy for militant black nationalist simply because they are Negroes. Third, these groups must be discredited in the eyes of Negro radicals, the followers of the movement. This last area requires entirely different tactics from the first two. Publicity about violent tendencies and radical statements merely enhances black nationalists to the last group; it adds "respectability" in a different way.

5. A final goal should be to prevent the long-range growth of militant black nationalist organizations, especially among youth. Specific tactics to prevent these groups from converting young people must be developed.

Besides these five goals counterintelligence is a valuable part of our regular investigative program as it often produces positive information.

TARGETS

Primary targets of the Counterintelligence Program, Black Nationalist-Hate Groups, should be the most violent and radical groups and their leaders. We should emphasize those leaders and organizations that are nationwide in scope and are most capable of disrupting this country. These targets should include the radical and violence-prone leaders, members, and followers of the:

Offices handling these cases and those of should be alert for counterintelligence suggestions.

INSTRUCTIONS

Within 30 days of the date of this letter each office should:

1. Advise the Bureau of the identity of the Special Agent assigned to coordinate this program.

the spaces censored by the bureau. This letter was issued one month before King was killed. Other Cointelpro files show that the FBI also had infiltrators operating within Malcolm's Muslim Mosque, Inc. (see chapter 5).

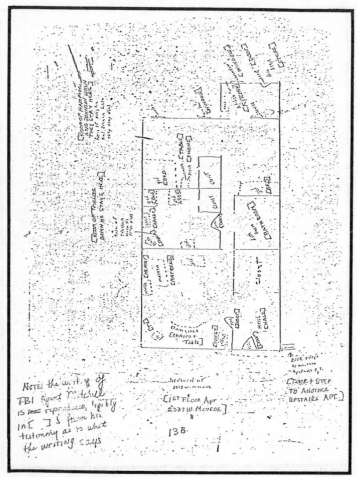

Detailed FBI floor plan of the Chicago apartment where Panther leaders Fred Hampton and Mark Clark were killed by police in 1969. An FBI agent made the drawing from information supplied by Hampton's bodyguard—who later surfaced as a bureau informer—and passed it on to Chicago police less than two weeks before the killings. A court ordered the files released in response to a suit by the victims' families.

24

Memorandum

TO : Mr. W. C. Sullivan   DATE: 10-9-69

FROM : C. D. Brennan

SUBJECT: SOCIALIST WORKERS PARTY (SWP)
INTERNAL SECURITY – SOCIALIST WORKERS PARTY
DISRUPTION PROGRAM

Purpose:

    To secure approval for discontinuance of our disruptive program against the SWP to eliminate paper work.

Observations:

    Captioned program was initiated on October 12, 1961 to cause disruption within the SWP and to alert the public to the organization's subversive character. Prior to October, 1967, this program was supervised as an adjunct of the Bureau's counterintelligence program directed against the communists, the Klan, and hate-type groups. Currently, this program is being supervised by the substantive desk responsible for handling the investigation of the SWP. Field is not required to submit status letters and potential counterintelligence actions are handled on an individual basis.

    Since the last evaluation of this program in October, 1968, four proposals have been considered with three being approved by the Bureau. No significant tangible results have been reported to date.

RECOMMENDATION:

    In order to eliminate paper work wherever possible, it is recommended that captioned disruptive action be discontinued as a program. In the future, the disruptive action directed against the SWP will be handled on an individual case basis as deemed appropriate

1 – Mr. W. C. Sullivan
1 – Mr. C. D. Brennan
1 – Mr. L. A. Crescioli

LAC:kle
(6)

Memos that ostensibly discontinued Cointelpro are worded unmistakably to allow future disruption. This one, dated October 10, 1969, recommends getting rid of the title "SWP Disruption Program" to "eliminate paper work," and adds: "In the future, the disruption action directed against the SWP will be handled on an individual case basis as deemed appropriate."

UNITED STATES GOVERNMENT

Memorandum

TO : Mr. W. C. Sullivan

FROM : Mr. C. D. Brennan

SUBJECT: COUNTERINTELLIGENCE PROGRAMS (COINTELPROS)
INTERNAL SECURITY - RACIAL MATTERS

DATE: 4/27/71

1 - Mr. Sullivan
1 - Mr. Brennan
1 - Mr. Branigan
1 - Mr. Gray
1 - Mr. G.C. Moore
1 - Mr. Shackelford
1 - Mr. Wannall
1 - Mr. Ryan

To afford additional security to our sensitive techniques and operations, it is recommended the COINTELPROS operated by the Domestic Intelligence Division be discontinued.

At the present time this Division operates seven COINTELPROS as follows:

COINTELPRO - Espionage
COINTELPRO - New Left
COINTELPRO - Disruption of White Hate Groups
COINTELPRO - Communist Party, USA
Counterintelligence and Special Operations
COINTELPRO - Black Extremists
Socialist Workers Party - Disruption Program

These programs involve a variety of sensitive intelligence techniques and disruptive activities which are afforded close supervision at the Seat of Government. They have been carefully supervised with all actions being afforded prior Bureau approval and an effort has been made to avoid engaging in harassment.. Although successful over the years, it is felt they should now be discontinued for security reasons because of their sensitivity.

In exceptional instances where counterintelligence action is warranted, it will be considered on a highly selective individual basis with tight procedures to insure absolute security.

ACTION:

If approved, attached airtel will be sent to all field offices discontinuing our COINTELPROS.

Enclosure
1 - 65-69260
1 - 100-449698
1 - 157-9
1 - 100-3-104
1 - 105-174254
1 - 100-448006
1 - 100-436291

EX-113   REC-39

Pages 26 and 27: 1971 documents purporting to end seven counterintelligence programs allude to the break-in at the Media, Pennsylvania, FBI office which shattered their secrecy. The programs "should now be discontinued for

26

4/28/71

1 - Mr. Sullivan
1 - Mr. Brennan
/Airtel   1 - Mr. Branigan
                                                     1 - Mr. Gray
                                                     1 - Mr. G.C. Moore
                                                     1 - Mr. Shackelford
To: SAC, Albany   PERSONAL ATTENTION   1 - Mr. Wannall
                                                     1 - Mr. Ryan
From: Director, FBI

COUNTERINTELLIGENCE PROGRAMS (COINTELPRO)
INTERNAL SECURITY - RACIAL MATTERS
O   -

        Effective immediately, all COINTELPROS operated
by this Bureau are discontinued. These include:

        COINTELPRO - Espionage
        COINTELPRO - New Left
        COINTELPRO - Disruption of White Hate Groups
        COINTELPRO - Communist Party, USA
        Counterintelligence and Special Operations
        COINTELPRO - Black Extremists
        Socialist Workers Party - Disruption Program

        In exceptional instances where it is considered
counterintelligence action is warranted, recommendations
should be submitted to the Bureau under the individual case
caption to which it pertains. These recommendations will
be considered on an individual basis.
                                              EX-103   REC-50 - 1518

        You are reminded that Bureau authority is required
before initiating any activity of a counterintelligence nature.

2 - All Field Offices (PERSONAL ATTENTION)

1 - 65-69260
1 - 100-449698
1 - 157-9   APR 30 1971
1 - 100-3-104
1 - 105-174254
1 - 100-443006
1 - 100-435291
DR:sfw
(336)

        See memorandum, same caption, dated 4/27/71, prepared

---

*security reasons," but disruptive tactics will continue "on a
highly selective individual basis with tight procedures to
insure absolute secrecy."*

"Symbolism and inspired leadership" are easy targets for the repressive institutions of the state, its propaganda agencies, and cooperative intellectuals. Solidly based organizations may be able to withstand such attacks. The same lesson, of course, must be learned outside the Black community.

We note further that the criminal activities of the FBI were initiated under the liberal Democratic administrations and carried further under Nixon. These programs were (partially) exposed during the Watergate period, and though incomparably more serious than anything charged against Nixon, they were virtually ignored during this period by the liberal national press and journals of opinion, and only marginally discussed since, though ample information is available. I have discovered personally—and others may verify for themselves—that much of the most significant information is unknown to generally well-informed journalists and other intellectuals, and that the scale of the FBI programs is rarely appreciated, though by now enough information is readily available for those who want to know.

We note finally that "the Justice Department has decided not to prosecute anyone in connection with the Federal Bureau of Investigation's 15-year campaign to disrupt the activities of suspected subversive organizations."[18] J. Stanley Pottinger, head of the Civil Rights Division, reported to the attorney general that he had found "no basis for criminal charges against any particular individuals involving particular incidents." The present director of the FBI has also made clear that he sees nothing particularly serious in the revelations of the past several years. There will be no Congressional committee conducting a serious investigation of these practices, and no furor in the liberal press over the revelations themselves or the failure to investigate them. In short, the system continues to work.

The criminal programs of the FBI during the 1960s are simply an extension of past practices. According to William C. Sullivan, Hoover's assistant for many years:

> Such a very great man as Franklin D. Roosevelt saw nothing wrong in asking the FBI to investigate those opposing his lend-lease policy—a purely political request. He also had us look into the activities of others who opposed our entrance into World War II, just as later Administrations had the FBI look into those opposing the conflict in Vietnam. It was a political request also when he [Roosevelt] instructed us to put a telephone tap, a microphone, and a physical surveillance on an internationally known leader in his

Administration. It was done. The results he wanted were secured and given to him. Certain records of this kind . . . were not then or later put into the regular FBI filing system. Rather, they were deliberately kept out of it.[19]

Not long after World War II ended, President Truman put into operation the repressive measures which laid the basis for what is misleadingly called "McCarthyism." The Mundt-Nixon bill calling for the registration of the Communist party was reported out of Nixon's House Committee on Un-American Activities in 1948. Senate liberals objected, and after a Truman veto they proposed as a substitute "the ultimate weapon of repression: concentration camps to intern potential troublemakers on the occasion of some loosely defined future 'Internal Security Emergency',"[20] including, as one case, "insurrection within the United States in aid of a foreign enemy."[21] This substitute was advocated by Benton, Douglas, Graham, Kefauver, Kilgore, Lehman, and Humphrey, then a freshman senator. Humphrey later voted against the bill, though he did not retreat from his concentration camp proposal. In fact, he was concerned that the conference committee had brought back "a weaker bill, not a bill to strike stronger blows at the Communist menace, but weaker blows." The problem with the new bill was that those interned in the detention centers would have "the right of habeas corpus so they can be released and go on to do their dirty business,"[22] Humphrey complained. In later years as well Senate liberals were responsible for some of the most repressive legislation.

During the same period, the ideological institutions of American society—the mass media, cinema, and the universities and schools—were successfully purified as radicals were largely eliminated from the sensitive professions and often harassed or dismissed elsewhere as well. It was only under the pressure of the student movement in the late 1960s that the universities were compelled to become slightly less orthodox and to make marginal concessions to freedom of thought and inquiry that moved beyond the ideological consensus determined by ruling groups. And even in those years, in numerous cases radicals were forced out of academic positions, often by faculty or administration decision, but in some instances over the heads of faculty and administrators, by the governing bodies of the universities.

It is now commonly argued that during the late 1960s the universities were virtually taken over by the left, while the mass media took on an adversary position with respect to state authority—some say irresponsibly, while others laud the press for its honesty and independence. This is gross nonsense. The orthodoxy of the universities was barely challenged. Overwhelmingly, university departments, particularly those concerned with domestic policy and international affairs, remained under the control of people committed to the reigning state capitalist ideology, and throughout the Vietnam War the subversion of the universities in the service of state policy persisted with only minor interference. As for the media, I have already pointed out that the Watergate affair—allegedly their finest hour—merely demonstrates their continued subservience to the ruling powers. The same is generally true with regard to the war in Vietnam. Even the liberal press generally continued, to the end, to describe the war as a conflict between North and South Vietnam, hewing close to the official propaganda line. Media doves joined most liberal intellectuals in protesting that the United States was defending South Vietnam in an exercise of misplaced benevolence. The war was "a mistake," a case of good motives transmuted (mysteriously) into bad policy, with no one to blame. The fact that the United States was engaged in direct aggression in South Vietnam, and that its murderous attack against the rural society of South Vietnam then spilled over to neighboring regions, has been consistently suppressed by the media and journals of opinion, again with a few honorable exceptions. The war in Laos and Cambodia was kept "secret" over long periods through the self-censorship of the press, which then hypocritically blamed Nixon for deception when the time came to punish him for his departure from the established rules of the game. Kissinger's efforts to evade the provisions of the "peace treaty" were also effectively kept from public attention, in a remarkable display of submissiveness. I have given elaborate documentation elsewhere, and will not discuss this matter further here.[23]

When someone suggests a reduction in military spending or the cancellation of some new superweapon development, outraged apologists for militarism are sure to denounce such proposals for "unilateral disarmament." Similarly, a slight breach in orthodoxy is sufficient to terrify authoritarian ideologues, who see in it the collapse of the system of thought control that has been so effective in depoliticizing American society. The gross exaggerations of frightened academics and political commentators serve to illustrate the extent and success of the long-standing system of ideological control in the United States.

I have spoken of this system as a post–World War II phenomenon, but that is a mistake. Its roots go far deeper. Recall that J. Edgar Hoover rose to national prominence when he was appointed chief of the General Intelligence (antiradical) division of the Justice Department in August 1919, just before the "Palmer raids" of January 2, 1920, when more than 4,000 alleged "radicals" were rounded up in thirty-three cities in twenty-three states (over 200 aliens were subsequently deported), while the *Washington Post* editorialized that "there is no time to waste on hairsplitting over infringement of liberty" in the face of the Bolshevik menace, and lauded the House of Representatives for its expulsion of socialist congressman Victor Berger on grounds that it could not have given a "finer or more impressive demonstration of Americanism"; the *New York Times* meanwhile described the expulsion of socialist assemblymen as "an American vote altogether, a patriotic and conservative vote" which "an immense majority of the American people will approve and sanction," whatever the benighted electorate may believe.[24]

One may trace the pattern back much further, to the Alien and Sedition Acts by which "the Federalists sought to suppress political opposition and to stamp out lingering sympathy for the principles of the French Revolution,"[25] or the judicial murder of four anarchists for "having advocated doctrines" which allegedly lay behind the explosion of a bomb in Chicago's Haymarket Square after a striker had been killed by police in May 1886.[26]

The Cointelpro documents and the related disclosures are noteworthy, and in accord with historical precedent, in that no specific illegal acts were charged against those "targeted" by the FBI, though a vague "propensity for violence" and unspecified violent acts are alleged. Similarly, the "seditious utterances" of the Haymarket anarchists sufficed, in the eyes of the Chicago police, to attribute "moral responsibility" for the bombing and to justify their prosecution and hanging.[27] And Attorney General Palmer justified his actions "to clean up the country almost unaided by any virile legislation" on grounds of the failure of Congress "to stamp out these seditious societies in their open defiance of law by various forms of propaganda":

> Upon these two basic certainties, first that the "Reds" were criminal aliens, and secondly that the American Government must prevent crime, it was decided that there could be no nice distinctions drawn between the theoretical ideals of the radicals and their actual violations of our national laws. . . .

Palmer's "information showed that communism in this country was an organization of thousands of aliens, who were direct allies of Trotsky." Thus "the Government is now sweeping the nation clean of such alien filth," with the overwhelming support of the press, until they perceived that their own interests were threatened.[28] Elsewhere he described the prisoners as follows:

Out of the sly and crafty eyes of many of them leap cupidity, cruelty, insanity, and crime; from their lopsided faces, sloping brows, and misshapen features may be recognized the unmistakable criminal type.

Palmer was a liberal and progressive. His purpose was "to tear out the radical seeds that have entangled American ideas in their poisonous theories."[30] His belief that the state has the authority to prevent these seeds from germinating is within the general framework of American liberalism. The mass media, the schools, and the universities defend ideological orthodoxy in their own, generally successful, ways. When a threat to reigning dogma is perceived, the state is entitled to act.

After World War I, labor militancy menaced established privilege. Hoover labored to portray the 1919 steel strike as a "Red conspiracy." A subsequent miner's strike was described by President Wilson as "one of the gravest steps ever proposed in this country," "a grave moral and legal wrong," while the press warned that the miners, "red-soaked in the doctrines of Bolshevism," were "starting a general revolution in America."[31] The Red Scare, as Levin shows, "was promoted, in large part, by major business groups which feared their power was threatened by a leftward trend in the labor movement"; and they had "reason to rejoice" at its substantial success, namely, "to weaken and conservatize the labor movement, to dismantle radical parties, and to intimidate liberals." It "was an attempt—largely successful—to reaffirm the legitimacy of the power elites of capitalism and to further weaken workers' class consciousness." The Red Scare was strongly backed by the press and the American elites until they came to see that their own interests would be harmed as the right-wing frenzy got out of hand—in particular, the anti-immigrant hysteria, which threatened the best reserve of cheap labor.

The Red Scare also served to buttress an interventionist foreign policy. Foster Rhea Dulles observed that "Governmental agencies made most of these fears and kept up a barrage of anti-Bolshevik propaganda throughout 1919 which was at least partially inspired by the need to justify the policy of intervention in both Archangel and Siberia."[32]

After World War II, the story was reenacted. While intellectual ideologists depicted American expansionism as "defense of freedom" (with an occasional, but so understandable excess of zeal), transmuting the brutal Russian state into a global aggressor under an elaborate mythology that even its creators have been compelled to disown, the state moved to ensure obedience and submissiveness to the evolving imperial system and the domestic permanent war economy. As already noted, American liberals had their hand in some of the worst abuses. The general motivation was the traditional one: "there could be no nice distinctions drawn between the theoretical ideals of the radicals and their actual violations of our national laws" (Palmer).

The basic liberal doctrine was laid out clearly by Supreme Court Justice Robert H. Jackson in his opinion upholding the Smith Act on grounds "that it was no violation of free speech to convict Communists for conspiring to teach or advocate the forcible overthrow of the government, even if no clear and present danger could be proved." For if the clear and present danger test were applied, Jackson argued, "it means that Communist plotting is protected during its period of incubation; its preliminary stages of organization and preparation are immune from the law; the Government can move only after imminent action is manifest, when it would, of course, be too late." Thus there must be "some legal formula that will secure an existing order against revolutionary radicalism. . . . There is no constitutional right to 'gang up' on the Government." Opposition tendencies, however minuscule, must be nipped in the bud prior to "imminent action." As for the Communist party, "ordinary conspiracy principles" suffice to charge any individual associated with it "with responsibility for and participation in all that makes up the Party's program" and "even an individual," acting alone and apart from any "conspiracy," "cannot claim that the Constitution protects him in advocating or teaching overthrow of government by force or violence. . . ."[33]

In conformity with these doctrines, the ideological institutions must be kept free of contamination. Even a single tenured Marxist professor of economics in a country as complex and diverse as the United States constitutes a potential threat. As in the case of the Red Scare of 1920, it was only when the hysteria that had been whipped up began to endanger major institutions and individuals near the center of power that the economic and political leadership and their intellectual spokesmen took effective measures to terminate the repression—or more accurately, to restrict it to the proper victims.

Given the historical context, it is entirely natural that the beginnings of the ferment of protest and organization in the early 1960s set the apparatus of repression into operation once again, in the manner described in the documents presented below and elsewhere. Nor is it surprising that American liberalism looked the other way, until the repression struck home under Nixon; and even then, it is important to emphasize once again, indignation was largely restricted to Nixon's crimes, insignificant in comparison to the revelations of the same period. Matters are no different when the Black anarchist Martin Sostre—designated as a "prisoner of conscience" by Amnesty International—is mercilessly persecuted by the state, or when Black students are murdered at Orangeburg and Jackson State, and on and on.

Some commentators have found it "puzzling" that the FBI should devote such energies to hounding a scoutmaster in Orange, New Jersey, whose wife is a socialist, or to disrupting small socialist parties, while "crime rates in American cities escalated and organized crime expanded its interests" and "the real espionage dangers from the Soviet K.G.B." were "apparently ignored."[34] Placing the events in their historical and doctrinal context, the puzzle is easily resolved. The real threat to the "existing order" is not organized crime or the KGB, but "revolutionary radicalism" or even protest by popular groups that have escaped the control of the political leadership and intellectual ideologists. That this threat can quickly become real indeed was made evident in the late 1960s, when American aggression in Vietnam was significantly hampered[35] and its ideological props swept away (in significant circles, though not in the major ideological institutions).

For the most part, however, the threat of intellectual independence and uncontrolled political and social organization has been well contained (the major postwar success of the "containment policy"). Alone among the parliamentary democracies, the United States has had no mass-based socialist party, however mild and reformist, no socialist voice in the media, and virtually no departure from centrist ideology within the schools and universities, at least until the pressure of student activism impelled a slight departure from orthodoxy. All of this is testimony to the effectiveness of the system of controls that has been in force for many years, the activities of the FBI being only the spearhead for far more extensive, substantial, and effective—if more low-keyed—measures enforced throughout American society.

From its inception, the FBI has operated on the liberal doctrine that "preliminary stages of organization and preparation" must be frustrated, well before there is any clear and present danger of "revolutionary radicalism," occasionally progressing beyond the intended bounds of this doctrine. The people of the United States pay dearly for domestic privilege and the securing of imperial domains. The vast waste of social wealth, miserable urban ghettos, meaningless work within authoritarian capitalist institutions, the threat (or reality) of loss of even the opportunity to rent oneself to the owners of capital, standards of health and social welfare that should be intolerable in a society with vast productive resources—all of this must be endured and even welcomed as "the price of freedom" if "the existing order" is to stand without challenge. The intelligentsia have generally played their natural role, promulgating the required doctrines with enthusiasm and energy and diverting or diluting any serious departure from the conventional system of beliefs, with an occasional show of dismay when privileged groups themselves are threatened. As for the state instruments of repression, one can expect little change in coming years, at least until the rise of mass-based popular organizations devoted to social change and to an end of oppression and injustice.

NOAM CHOMSKY
July 1975

Notes

1. Henry Steele Commager, "The Constitution is Alive and Well," *New York Times,* August 11, 1974. Commager, who has been forceful in defense of civil liberties and opposition to the Indochina war, states that prior to Nixon, "no President has ever attempted to subvert" the Constitution or "challenged the basic assumptions of our constitutional system itself." But "the system worked" and the challenge was defeated.

2. Press release of the Department of Justice, released by Attorney

General William B. Saxbe and FBI Director Clarence M. Kelley, November 18, 1974.

3. See *New York Times,* August 4, 1974, for documents and commentary.

4. John M. Crewdson, "Levi Reveals more Harassment by F.B.I.," *New York Times,* May 24, 1975. Also, Associated Press, *Boston Globe,* May 24, 1975.

5. On the latter, see Vin McLellan, "FBI Heists Names of 1970 Student Strikers," *Boston Phoenix,* March 5, 1974, based on the report of former security officers at Brandeis University.

6. John M. Crewdson, "Black Pastor Got F.B.I. Threat in '69," *New York Times,* March 17, 1965.

7. For a review of some of these actions, see Dave Dellinger, *More Power than We Know* (New York, Doubleday, 1975); Gary T. Marx, "Thoughts on a Neglected Category of Social Movement Participant: The Agent Provocateur and the Informant," *American Journal of Sociology,* vol. 80, no. 2 (September 1974), pp. 402-42. See also Steven V. Roberts, "F.B.I. Informer Is Linked to Right-Wing Violence," *New York Times,* June 24, 1974, and Everett R. Holles, "A.C.L.U. Says F.B.I. Funded 'Army' To Terrorize Antiwar Protesters," *New York Times,* June 27, 1975, for some examples of FBI operations in San Diego, ranging from "espionage, vandalism and mail theft to bombings, assassination plots and shootings, according to the report" filed by the ACLU for the Senate Select Committee on Intelligence. The report cites the testimony of an FBI informer that he was instructed to assassinate Peter Bohmer in the winter of 1971-72, though the attempt was not carried out. But in January 1972, shots were fired into Bohmer's house, wounding an occupant, by members of the Secret Army Organization, set up (according to the report) "on instructions of F.B.I. officials," and an FBI agent identified in court as the "control" for the organization hid the gun used in the attack for nearly six months. Bohmer was, meanwhile, hounded out of his position at San Diego State University and was, for a time, committed to a hospital for the criminally insane for observation after his participation in civil disobedience against the war.

8. Mike Royko, *Chicago Daily News; Boston Globe,* February 1, 1975. Royko's source refused to take his information to the investigating agencies, on the grounds that "these local prosecutors . . . were involved in the same kind of thing" and will "wind up looking at themselves in a mirror."

9. For information on these and other FBI actions in Seattle, see Dellinger, *op. cit.,* and Frank J. Donner, "Hoover's Legacy," *The Nation,* June 1, 1974.

10. John M. Crewdson, "Ex-Operative Says He Worked For F.B.I. To Disrupt Political Activities Up To '74," *New York Times,* February 24, 1975.

11. *Civil Liberties,* No. 273, December 1970; publication of the ACLU.

12. Dellinger, *op. cit.*

13. John Kifner, "F.B.I. Gave Chicago Police Plan of Slain Panther's Apartment," *New York Times,* May 25, 1974. Although the fact of FBI involvement in the Hampton assassination, along with other details of this major state crime, was not widely publicized outside of Chicago, nevertheless there were a few reports, such as this one. There can be no excuse for the general silence on this matter, which alone overshadows the entire Watergate affair by a substantial margin.

14. John Kifner, "Security Aide for Indians Says He Was F.B.I. Informer," *New York Times,* March 13, 1975.

15. *Special Report of Interagency Committee on Intelligence* (Ad Hoc), Chairman, J. Edgar Hoover, along with the directors of the CIA, DIA, and NSA, prepared for the President, June 25, 1970, marked "Top Secret." A censored version was later released. Quotes below are from Book 7, Part 1: *Summary of Internal Security Threat.*

16. For analysis and texts of the Media documents, see Paul Cowan, Nick Egleson, and Nat Hentoff, *State Secrets* (Holt, Rinehart and Winston, 1973). Comparable figures are given by Marx (*op. cit.*). He notes that "among the 34 cases [of infiltration] for which some information is available, 11 involved white campus groups; 11, predominantly white peace groups and/or economic groups; 10, black and Chicano groups; and only two, right-wing groups." Furthermore, "in two-thirds of the 34 cases considered here, the specious activists appear to have gone beyond passive information gathering to active provocation."

17. C. Gerald Fraser, "F.B.I. Action in 1961 Called Still Harmful to Hopes of Blacks," *New York Times,* April 6, 1974. See also Jesse Jackson and Alvin F. Poussaint, "The Danger Behind FBI Obstruction of Black Movements," *Boston Globe,* April 2, 1974.

18. "Charges Over F.B.I.'s Tactics on Subversive Suspects Barred," *Washington Star-News; New York Times,* January 4, 1975.

19. Letter to the annual Chief Justice Earl Warren Conference on Advocacy, June 7-8, 1974, cited from the final report, *Privacy in a Free Society,* by Nat Hentoff, "The Privacy War Games," *The Village Voice,* December 9, 1974.

20. Frank Wilkinson, *The Era of Libertarian Repression—1948 to 1973: from Congressman to President, with Substantial Support from the Liberal Establishment,* University of Akron, 1974; reprinted from the *University of Akron Law Review.*

21. Emergency Detention Act of 1950, cited by Wilkinson.

22. Cited by Wilkinson from *96 Congressional Record,* 1950, 15520-1.

23. See my *For Reasons of State* (Pantheon, 1973) and earlier books. Also my "Reporting Indochina: the News Media and the Legitimation of Lies," *Social Policy,* October 1973; "The Remaking of History," *Ramparts,* August 1975. See also (with E.S. Herman) *Counterrevolutionary Violence: Bloodbaths in Fact and Propaganda* (Warner Modular, 1973), suppressed by order of the parent conglomerate (Warner Brothers) but available in French (*Bains de Sang,* Seghers/Laffont, 1974) and other European languages. It should be noted that there was a fair amount of honest and

important work by foreign correspondents in the field, and occasional instances of accurate and serious review and analysis at the editorial level as well. For an outstanding example, see the review of the war in the special supplement of the *St. Louis Post-Dispatch* under the direction of Richard Dudman, April 30, 1975.

24. On the post–World War I "Red Scare" see Murray B. Levin, *Political Hysteria in America: the Democratic Capacity for Repression* (Basic Books, 1971). Other sources have cited figures as high as 10,000 arrested during the Palmer Raids and 700 aliens deported. See Max Lowenthal, *The Federal Bureau of Investigation* (William Sloane Associates, Inc., 1950).

25. David Brion Davis, editor, *The Fear of Conspiracy* (Cornell University Press, 1971).

26. *Ibid.* A fifth committed suicide before the sentence of death could be executed. Three others were sentenced to hanging as well, but were not executed. No proof was offered that any of the eight had been involved in the bomb-throwing.

27. See the excerpt from Michael J. Schaack, *Anarchy and Anarchists,* Chicago, 1889, in Davis's collection. Schaack was captain of the East Chicago Avenue Police Station and "was widely credited with having uncovered the anarchist conspiracy" (Davis).

28. See excerpts from Palmer in Davis, *op cit.* On the role of the press, see Levin, *op cit.*

29. Cited by Levin.

30. See excerpt in Davis, *op. cit.*

31. Cf. Levin, *op. cit.*

32. Foster Rhea Dulles, *The Road to Teheran* (Princeton, 1945), cited by Levin, *op. cit.*

33. See the concurring and dissenting opinions of Mr. Justice Jackson cited in Davis, *op. cit.*

34. Nicholas M. Horrock, "The F.B.I.'s Appetite for Very Small Potatoes," *New York Times,* March 23, 1975.

35. On the significance of the threat, both actual and potential, as perceived at high levels of policy planning, see my review of some of the evidence contained in the "Pentagon Papers" in *For Reasons of State,* chapter 1. For discussion of the impact on the American expeditionary force, see David Cortright, *Soldiers in Revolt,* (New York, Doubleday, 1975).

1 'Prevent these people from getting elected'

In late 1971 Donald Segretti was discharged from the army, where he had served as an attorney. He had a friend in the White House and he quickly landed a new job.

In the next few months strange things began to happen to some of the candidates for the Democratic presidential nomination. During the New Hampshire primary the state's major newspaper printed a letter accusing Edmund Muskie of making derogatory statements about French-Americans. Sometime later it would be discovered that the letter was a phony, but two weeks before election day it sparked quite a stir.

Later, there were fake press releases issued on the stationery of Muskie and Hubert Humphrey.

Then, on June 17, 1972, five men were discovered breaking into the headquarters of the Democratic National Committee at the Watergate complex in Washington, D.C. The story that eventually unraveled—including spying and political sabotage—had an unprecedented impact on American political life. It eventually forced the resignation of the president of the United States.

The Cointelpro documents reveal that none of the Watergate crimes were original. The FBI has for years been doing the same thing—and worse—to the Socialist Workers party. Every one of the plumbers' "dirty tricks" had been used for years by the FBI against the SWP, civil rights leaders, and others on the government's "enemies list."

As this country's political police, the FBI has been assigned the role of determining what ideas are fit for the American people to hear and what ideas are not. Socialism, in their opinion, is not fit.

The ruling class, which runs the government, is convinced that it would be better for them if socialism were considered illegitimate or "subversive." The idea that the working people of this country should take over its wealth and resources and use them for their own welfare is a subversive idea—if you are a capitalist.

In the early 1960s the witch-hunt that had dominated American politics during the 1950s was giving way to a greater openness to radical ideas. Socialists began winning a place on the ballot—and were more and more being treated as legitimate candidates with a particular point of view. The FBI decided that they had a problem. Cointelpro was their solution.

The Cointelpro plot to disrupt socialist election campaigns was concocted not because of any illegal activities by the SWP, but because, as J. Edgar Hoover said, socialist candidates were "openly" talking to people about their ideas.

The documents at the end of this chapter show that the FBI attempted to wreck the 1961 campaign of a Black socialist for Manhattan borough president, waged a sustained drive against Clifton DeBerry, the SWP's 1964 presidential candidate, tried to get socialists excluded from supporting an independent Black candidate in San Francisco in 1964, and incited an attack on Fred Halstead when he was the SWP presidential candidate in 1968.

These actions are only part of the record of FBI sabotage against socialist candidates. And there are operations that remain hidden in files the FBI is refusing to disclose.

One Cointelpro operation that has come to light through the socialists' suit concerns the 1966 campaign of Judy White for governor of New York. This was during the period when the antiwar movement was beginning to have a major impact on the thinking of the American people. White was a leader of the antiwar movement.

A broad layer of opponents of the war—including many radicals who were not particularly close to the SWP—had endorsed White as the only antiwar candidate in the race.

Campaign supporters worked hard to get the signatures necessary to obtain ballot status, which brought a significant amount of attention from the media.

The FBI looked for a way to sabotage this campaign. They noticed that according to New York law White was formally not old enough to hold the office of governor. The FBI tried to get this fact reported in the media in an attempt to discredit the campaign.

According to the documents, the FBI decided to rely on the *Daily News* to do the job for them, but the New York City CBS television affiliate did it instead. A copy of the transcript of the editorial broadcast by the station immediately following the election is reproduced in the files.

White recently read the Cointelpro papers relating to her campaign. "It was the CBS editorial that started the whole controversy that led to the passage of what was called the 'anti-Judy White law,'" she recalled.

As the documents show, the state legislature soon passed a law altering the election code to require that a candidate be old enough to assume an office in order to run for it.

"Even before the election, CBS was making effective use of the charge that I wasn't 'old enough.' I'm sure the FBI must have planted this idea," White said.

"We were getting many hours of broadcast time, which was uncommon then. But a few days before the elections it abruptly stopped."

"I was scheduled to go on CBS with the other candidates for governor on a special one-hour program. Suddenly, CBS informed us that my appearance was canceled. They said I was not a legally qualified candidate because of my age."

Of course, White was legally qualified to run for office; that was why the law was changed. Today people under thirty are legally ineligible to run for governor of New York.

These documents indicate that the FBI may have been responsible for getting this legislation on the books.

The next set of documents concerns an FBI undercover plot implemented the previous year. The city was Denver, where the Socialist Workers party was fielding candidates in the elections for school board.

"In an effort to prevent these people from being elected," the Denver office proposed to FBI headquarters that a letter be sent to the president of the Denver school board to "alert" him to the fact that socialists were running for positions on the board.

The Denver FBI included in its proposal to Washington an article about the SWP that had appeared in the *Denver Post* the previous year. That article branded the SWP "as both subversive and on the Attorney General's list of subversive organizations." The FBI likes the media to refer to the SWP in this fashion, and there is every reason to believe that the FBI was involved in writing that story.

(The attorney general's list, a McCarthy-era compilation of "subversive" organizations, was officially abolished by Nixon during his last days in office. However, the government still maintains a secret list of "subversive organizations" for use by government agencies.)

The FBI seemed to be irritated because the Denver press had failed to label the SWP as subversive when the party announced its school board candidates.

Washington gave the go-ahead for a letter from "a concerned mother."

The next group of documents exposes an FBI operation aimed at a Black socialist. The FBI tried to ruin Paul Boutelle's campaign for mayor of New York in 1969 and to drive him and other Blacks out of the SWP.

The FBI discovered through its surveillance of the SWP that Boutelle had been arrested in New Jersey and falsely charged with possession of stolen property while he was helping a friend to move. The FBI sought to exploit this by circulating information on the arrest to the press.

While no New York newspaper ever printed the story, the FBI indicates in a document printed here that the information might have been passed on to supporters of Mayor John Lindsay, who was running for reelection, thus encouraging them to challenge the petitions the SWP had submitted in order to obtain ballot status.

This challenge resulted in the board of elections ruling the SWP off the ballot, and the party was forced to run a write-in campaign. If this was caused by the FBI, as they suggest, that makes this one of the more successful Cointelpro operations.

The second part of the plot was less successful. The FBI followed up by mailing Boutelle a racist letter, purportedly from a white member of the SWP, attacking him for both the arrest and remarks Boutelle had made at an earlier SWP convention.

The effect of this letter, as recorded in FBI files and as recalled by members of the SWP who were in New York in 1969, is instructive.

The FBI has made other political organizations the target of this type of disruption with some success, but these tactics do not prove very useful against a politically seasoned and experienced organization like the SWP.

Boutelle brought the letter directly to the attention of a meeting of the New York SWP, where it could be openly discussed. Party members immediately spotted the letter as the work of police. "We've been through this before," the FBI quotes one member as saying. "No one in the SWP wrote that."

*   *   *

There are those who are horrified by the Watergate crimes, yet feel that the use of the same tactics against socialists is excusable in the name of "national security." They accept the notion that certain ideas and the advocates of those ideas are beyond the pale.

One of the main lessons of both Watergate and the Cointelpro papers is that the use of such illegal methods against political opponents cannot remain limited to socialists. If tolerated, they will inevitably be aimed at other forces in this society who run into conflict with the powers that be. This is an important conclusion to be drawn by the labor movement and others.

SUBJECT : SOCIALIST WORKERS PARTY
INTERNAL SECURITY – SWP
DISRUPTION PROGRAM

Re Bureau letter to New York, October 12, 1961,
captioned as above.

The following are suggestions regarding initiating
a Socialist Workers Party (SWP) Disruption Program on a
limited basis:

1. Referenced Bureau letter states the SWP has,
over the past several years, been openly espousing its line
on a local and national basis through running candidates for
public office. Letters to newspaper editors and other various
columns in newspapers publishing letters from subscribers
could be mailed to newspapers, signed by fictitious names,
and pointing out that at the same time these individuals are
candidates for political office in the United States they are
members of the SWP, an organization dedicated to the revolutionary overthrow of the United States Government. The fact that
they are SWP candidates indicates that they are SWP members.
Information from public sources could be pooled from all
offices indicating the anarchist and revolutionary basis of the
SWP. The fact that the SWP has been cited by the Attorney
General of the United States as a subversive organization could
be fully outlined. This fact is probably not as generally known
as it should be. This procedure would alert the public to the
fact that in voting for a SWP candidate they are not voting for
an innocuous "Socialist" candidate or a "labor" candidate but
for a candidate dedicated to the overthrow of the United States
Government.

The above idea of labeling the SWP as a subversive
organization, which it is, could be expanded upon and other
means of adequately publishing this fact utilized. Leaflets
outlining the above could be mimeographed and surreptitiously

*Pages 44 and 45: Initial suggestions for disruption tactics
against the SWP submitted by the Detroit office in
November 1961, less than a month after Hoover's directive*

left at polling places. The information could be forwarded
to newspaper reporters, radio and television stations, always
taking necessary precautions so that the identity of the FBI
as the source would not be disclosed.

      2. With regard to the SWP supporting causes such
as CASTRO'S Cuba and groups concerned with integration
problems in the south, it is known that the SWP to a certain
extent dominates the Fair Play for Cuba Committee, is
attempting to dominate and control the Committee to Aid the
Monroe Defendants and is seeking sponsors for this latter
organization. The following ideas ~~could be utilized:~~ could be utilized:

      a. Letters could be mailed to the sponsors of such
organizations outlining the subversive connections of the
officers of the organizations and advising them as to the nature
of the organization that they are sponsoring. This might cause
sponsors to publicly withdraw their support.

      b. When organizations such as above rent halls for
meetings and so forth, information regarding the real nature
of the organization and the subversive connections of its
leaders could by various means be channeled to the management
of the halls so that they will refuse to rent the hall to the
organization. This could be repeated causing the disruption
of proposed meetings.

      c. Reporters, newspapers and other media could be
informed regarding the subversive affiliations of the leaders
of these organizations with the hope that they will publicize
this information (for example ED SHAW, Midwest Regional Director
of the Fair Play for Cuba Committee is a SWP member).

      Locally the Detroit Office will use the ideas and
methods ~~fitted to and implemented by ideas and methods appropriate~~
fitted to and implemented by ideas and methods appropriate
for the limited SWP membership. However, prior Bureau approval
will be obtained by any new counter-intelligence operations.
FOR

- 2 -

*launching the program. The proposals center on the use of
the "subversive" label to smear the party and any causes it
was supporting.*

DIRECTOR, FBI ⟨⟩   DATE: 10/24/66

SAC, NEW YORK ⟨⟩

SOCIALIST WORKERS PARTY
IS-SWP
DISRUPTION PROGRAM

As the Bureau is aware, the Socialist Workers Party (SWP) is currently running candidates in the forthcoming election in the State of New York. JUDY WHITE heads the SWP ticket as candidate for Governor.

It is known that WHITE was chosen for this role since the Party desired a youthful candidate who had participated in the anti-war movement, and who would campaign on this issue and appeal to individuals of this ilk.

It is further known that the Party, in choosing WHITE, was aware that she did not meet the residency requirement for holding such office, however, felt that if this was challenged the Party would compare WHITE's New York residency status with that of ROBERT KENNEDY, and the resultant publicity would outweigh any turn of events including WHITE's removal from the ballot. The Party had an old time member standing in the wings to replace WHITE if such occurred.

Therefore, to date, utilization of this information has not been recommended under this program.

It appears at this time, however, that a good possibility for disruption exists if this information was publicly released at election time making a comparison with JOHN CLARENCE FRANKLIN, a previous Party candidate. It is believed this could be accomplished in a humorous vein and released at the time of election when Party rebuttal would be useless.

A Xerox copy of a public release concerning FRANKLIN, effected under this program, is attached.

Pages 46-49: In 1966, the FBI attempted to undermine Judy White's campaign for governor of New York by getting the press to publicize the fact that if elected she would not meet the age requirement for holding that office. In the memo on page 49 the bureau takes credit for helping inspire the

The following example is submitted for the Bureau's consideration in furnishing this information to the friendly writer of the NYC newspaper which previously published the attached article:

"HER SLIP IS SHOWING....

Proud of my reputation as an independent thinker, I may once again hop, skip and jump over the voting machine. My choice for Governor, as leader of the ticket, should reflect the utmost consideration as to which candidate will do the best job. The choice, however, is made a little easier by the presence on the ballot of JUDY WHITE, candidate for Governor on the ticket of the Socialist Workers Party. JUDY's platform indicates that, if elected, she will crusade for a voting age of 18; however, her own age of 28 would preclude her serving, even if elected. Seems there are only three requirements for this job in the State Constitution, to wit: a U.S. citizen, attainment of 30 years of age, residency in New York for five years immediately preceding election. Her residency in New York for less than six months also appears to leave something to be desired. The Socialist Workers Party seems to have a flair for running curious candidates as evidenced by JOHN CLARENCE FRANKLIN, its 1961 candidate for president of the borough of Manhattan. JOHN's arrest record ran from petty larceny to first degree murder and later received free room and board in Clinton Prison. How such candidates manage a spot on the ballot is interesting speculation. Do you get the impression its leg-pulling time?"

The NYO feels that publication of the above information, in the manner recommended, would seriously and effectively embarrass the SWP. It would, furthermore, spotlight another example of the Party's ineptness and lack of serious-mindedness in its efforts to influence others. It is, therefore, felt that this latest exposure could result in another "nail in the coffin" of the Party in the eyes of other radical groups, together with unaffiliated individuals who might be swayed by the Party line.

-2-

"Anti-Judy White Law" barring young people from the ballot. The reference to John Clarence Franklin on page 46 concerns an earlier FBI operation against a Black socialist candidate, which is described in chapter 4.

Editorial '02

CBS-TV, 51 WEST 52 STREET, NEW YORK, N.Y. 10019

WCBS-TV Editorials express the views of the station's management on important community issues. Because opinions on these issues may differ, WCBS-TV will consider requests for time on the station for representing differing views: CLARK D. GEORGE, Vice President, CBS Television Stations Division and General Manager, WCBS-TV.

SUBJECT:	ELECTION LAW REFORM
SPOKESMAN:	Michael F. Keating
BROADCAST:	November 18, 1966 6 PM Evening Report November 21, 1966 7 AM Morning Report

In covering the recent elections in New York, we discovered what we consider to be a serious flaw in our election law, a flaw that should be corrected immediately. And the flaw is that, under the present system, a person can run for governor or other state offices even though that person may not be eligible to serve if elected, according to the provisions of our state Constitution.

For example, the state Constitution says that in order to serve as governor, a person must be 30 years old, a resident of the state for the five years preceding the election, and a United States citizen. But, the Secretary of State tells us, there is no procedure that calls for an automatic check to determine that a candidate nominated for governor meets those qualifications.

Now, in the past election, the Socialist Worker Party candidate for governor was a woman named Judith White. But if she had been elected, according to the Constitution she could not have served, because she is 28 years old. And, as I mentioned, the state Constitution says that the governor must be at least 30.

Since the Constitution does contain certain qualifications for the office of governor, then the same qualifications should apply to the people who run for that office. It doesn't make sense to have a candidate running for an office that the Constitution says he is not eligible to fill. Everyone who votes for that candidate throws his vote away, and, in a tight race, those votes could be crucial. If that candidate should happen to win election, it could result in a breakdown of our government.

In our opinion, the law should ensure that candidates on the ballot are eligible to serve in the office for which they are running.

* * *

We would like to remind our viewers that WCBS-TV will consider requests for time for the presentation of views differing from those expressed in our editorials.

Memorandum

DIRECTOR, FBI (100-436291)   DATE: 5/5/67

SAC, NEW YORK (100-146608)

CT: SOCIALIST WORKERS PARTY
IS–SWP
DISRUPTION PROGRAM

ReNYlets to Director, 10/24/66 and 1/20/67.

Relets concerned the suggested disruptive
tactic of publicizing the ineligibility of the
SWP's candidate for Governor of New York State
during 1966, which suggestion was accepted by the
Bureau and furnished to the "New York Daily News"
by Crime Record Division. No subsequent publication
of this information was noted in this New York City
newspaper, however, a Columbia Broadcasting System
(CBS) editorial subsequently appeared on television
on 11/18/66, which contained allegations similar to
those furnished New York City newspapers. Although
it has not been definitely established it is suspected
by the New York Office CBS may have received this
information from the "New York Daily News." For
the information of the Bureau the State of New York
recently passed a law which would nullify any future
instance of ineligible candidates running for public
office.

It is noted that "New York Times," 4/23/67,
contained an article on page 75, which stated that the
"anti-Judy White bill" which barred an ineligible
person from being nominated for public office has
been signed by New York State Governor NELSON ROCKEFELLER.
It was disclosed that New York State Attorney General
LOUIS J. LEFKOWITZ drafted this bill which was
sponsored by New York State Senator EDWARD J. SPENO,
Nassau County Republican chairman. The article noted
that WHITE running as Gubernatorial candidate for the
SWP received 12,506 votes out of 6.1 million cast.

F B I

Date: 5/4/65

Transmit the following in

Via ___ AIRTEL

TO: DIRECTOR, FBI

FROM: SAC, DENVER

SUBJECT: COMMUNIST PARTY, USA
           COUNTERINTELLIGENCE PROGRAM
           INTERNAL SECURITY — C
           (SOCIALIST WORKERS PARTY)

Re Denver letter 4/20/65 and Bureau letter 4/28/65, captioned as above.

Enclosed for the Bureau is one copy each of articles appearing in the 4/25/65 issue of the "Denver Post" and 5/4/65 issue of the "Rocky Mountain News" concerning upcoming Denver school board election.

Referenced Denver letter contained information that ALLEN TAPLIN, Branch Organizer of the Denver Branch, SWP, was running for the Denver School Board, which election is being held 5/18/65. However, BARBARA TAPLIN and HOWARD WALLACE, both members of the Denver Branch, SWP, have filed their candidacy for election to the school board instead of ALLEN TAPLIN as previously reported.

Bureau authority is requested prior to 5/11/65 for Denver to send the revised suggested letter and enclosed newspaper clippings to the President of the Denver School Board in an effort to prevent these people from being elected.

The suggested letter is as follows:

Pages 50 and 51: In 1965 the Denver office of the FBI outlined a scheme to send a fake letter from "a concerned mother" giving ammunition for red-baiting of a socialist

"Dear Sir:

"Recently while discussing with a friend
the various candidates for the upcoming Denver
School Board Election, I observed the names of
Mrs. Barbara Taplin, 1631 Pearl Street, and
Howard Wallace, 1860 Race Street, Denver, Colo-
rado as candidates for the Denver School Board
with their political parties listed as SWP.

"I vividly recall that Mr. Allen Taplin
who is listed in the 'Post' article dated
4/25/65 as the husband of Mrs. Barbara Taplin,
as the unsuccessful Socialist Workers Party
candidate for the United States House of
Representatives in 1964. In an article of
the 'Denver Post' which I am enclosing for your
information, this organization is listed as
both subversive and on the Attorney General's
list of subversive organizations. The article
also hints that Mr. Taplin is a communist.

"Being a conscientious voter and mother of
school age children, I feel that someone should
do something to prevent persons of this sort
from being elected to the school board.

"Although I am much in favor of publicly
opposing these people, I feel it best for my
family's sake that I withhold my name and leave
this situation in your capable hands.

"A Concerned Mother"

If authority is granted to mail this letter, Bureau
instructions concerning previous approved letter will be
followed.

school board candidate. The aim is clearly stated: "to
prevent these people from being elected." Washington
approved the operation.

of the SWP signatures were invalid. According to the "Daily
News", because the SWP had filed before LINDSAY's Independent
Party, it won a top-line position on the ballot. Thus LINDSAY,
the Liberal Party nominee, by challenging the SWP petition
was making "a bid to win a second top line on the Nov. 4 ballot".

On 9/19/69, "The New York Times" reported that, "The
Socialist Workers Party was removed yesterday from the ballot
in the city-wide November elections when the Board of Elections
ruled that most of the signatures on its petition were invalid"
.... and this action "virtually assured Mayor LINDSAY a second
top spot on the voting machines for his Independent Party".

It is not known to what extent the information regarding BOUTELLE's arrest, if known to LINDSAY supporters, encouraged
them to challenge the SWP petition. In any event, the SWP
political campaign has been disrupted in New York.

In an effort to further polarize blacks and whites
within the SWP, and particularly to further irritate BOUTELLE
over the "racism" within the Party, Bureau authority is requested
to prepare the following anonymous letter on commercial stationery
for transmittal to BOUTELLE at his home address, 2159 Davidson
Ave., Bronx, NY:

"'Comrade' Paul"

"Some of us within the Party are fed up with
the subversive effect you are having on the Party,
but since a few see your presence as an asset
(because of your color only) not much can be said
openly.

"Your racist remarks at the Convention show
you to be utterly useless to the revolution to come.
And then, as could have been expected, you and your
friends have put the Party in a position of possibly
having to defend a common thief.

"Why don't you and the rest of your fellow
party monkeys hook up with the Panthers where you'd
feel at home?

- 3 -

*Pages 52-54: The New York FBI office was unsuccessful in
its efforts to publicize the fact that Paul Boutelle had been
arrested on trumped-up charges, but claimed part of the
credit for getting him ruled off the ballot in the 1969 New-
York mayoral election. Washington approved New York's*

"Maybe then we could get on with the job Trotsky had in mind for us.

"Your 'nasty' friends".

Since confidential sources feel tnat BOUTELLE is merely being "used" because of his color, and his Convention remarks indicate he might be aware of this fact, it is expected that BOUTELLE may become more outspoken regarding racism within the Party, all of which would create some diversion within its ranks, and could result in BOUTELLE's resignation and conceivably other Negroes with whom BOUTELLE is friendly.

If authority is granted to prepare and mail the above letter, all precautions will be taken to insure the mailing cannot be associated with the FBI.

- 4 -

proposal to send a racist letter, ostensibly from a white member, to "polarize blacks and whites within the SWP" and demoralize Boutelle. The reason for the operation (page 54) is the bureau's complaint that the party is "growing rapidly" and running candidates for office.

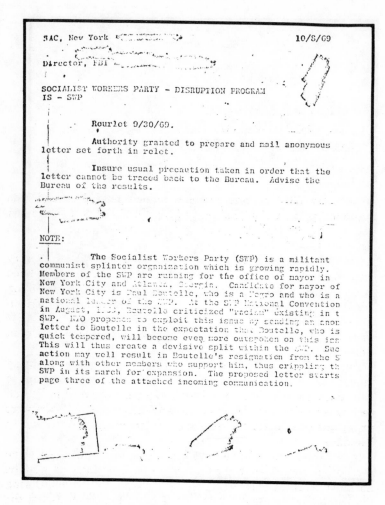

SAC, New York ⟨⟩ 10/8/69

Director, FBI

SOCIALIST WORKERS PARTY - DISRUPTION PROGRAM
IS - SWP

Reurlet 9/30/69.

Authority granted to prepare and mail anonymous
letter set forth in relet.

Insure usual precaution taken in order that the
letter cannot be traced back to the Bureau. Advise the
Bureau of the results.

NOTE:

The Socialist Workers Party (SWP) is a militant
communist splinter organization which is growing rapidly.
Members of the SWP are running for the office of mayor in
New York City and Atlanta, Georgia. Candidate for mayor of
New York City is Paul Boutelle, who is a Negro and who is a
national leader of the SWP. At the SWP National Convention
in August, 1969, Boutelle criticized "racism" existing in t
SWP. NYO proposes to exploit this issue by sending an anon
letter to Boutelle in the expectation that Boutelle, who is
quick tempered, will become even more outspoken on this iss
This will thus create a devisive split within the SWP. Suc
action may well result in Boutelle's resignation from the S
along with other members who support him, thus crippling th
SWP in its march for expansion. The proposed letter starts
page three of the attached incoming communication.

54

2 Inciting violence: 'It should be an interesting experience for Mr. Halstead'

Early in 1946 a young sailor named Fred Halstead was stationed on a ship off the coast of China. World War II had just ended, but on the mainland of China the fighting had not stopped. A civil war was raging.

Back in Washington the rulers of this country were very interested in the outcome of that struggle. They would have liked to send their army in to back up Chiang Kai-shek's crumbling forces, but their attempts to stall the demobilization of American troops after the war provoked massive protests among the GIs. It was clear that large-scale U.S. military intervention in China was out of the question.

Two decades later when the United States began committing thousands of troops to another Asian country in an attempt to hold back a revolution, Fred Halstead remembered what he had seen while he was in the navy. He was convinced that there were important lessons for the growing movement against the war in Vietnam.

In an interview, Halstead talked about this and about some revelations contained in the Cointelpro papers. Halstead was the Socialist Workers party candidate for president in 1968. During the campaign he made a trip to Vietnam. It now turns out the FBI had tried to sabotage that trip.

Among the documents turned over to the SWP under federal court order is evidence that the FBI wrote a "news story" that it sought to have placed in the military press.

The FBI's purpose was to provoke violence against the socialist presidential candidate during his visit to Vietnam. "It should be an interesting experience for Mr. HALSTEAD when he encounters the men who have served both their own country and others in the interest of freedom," the FBI's article concluded.

Before discussing that experience, Halstead described what he had seen at the close of the Second World War.

"I was attached to a ship that was part of the Seventh Fleet in Chinese waters. Ostensibly, we were there to repatriate Japanese troops," Halstead said.

"But after unloading our passengers in Japan, we found ourselves loading up again. This time with Chinese troops, which we took up to a port in northern China. This was part of the use of the American navy to assist Chiang's offensive in the Chinese civil war.

"Well, most of us didn't know there was such a thing as a civil war in China until we found ourselves more or less involved in it."

The GIs had just finished one war, and they didn't like the idea of getting into another one. Soon a protest movement developed.

"I remember walking into the Red Cross building in Shanghai where GIs would go to get coffee and hamburgers," Halstead said. "There I saw this big banner with the words: 'GIs Unite! We want to go home!'"

There were mimeograph machines aboard the ships and on the army posts, and leaflets expressing that demand were reproduced. "I didn't organize all this, but I picked up leaflets and passed them out," Halstead recalled.

He also remembers attending meetings where some of the organizers gave speeches condemning imperialism. "But mainly, it was a movement of GIs who just wanted to go home."

They held some big demonstrations. There was one in Manila and another in Shanghai. The message got through, and orders soon came in to return to the United States.

"This made an impression on me that I didn't forget. That you could organize among GIs," Halstead remarked. "Just that simple proposition."

When he got back home, Halstead had some additional experiences that he later found useful in the antiwar movement. He went to work as a civilian seaman in the merchant marine, where he was a member of the Sailors' Union of the Pacific. But before long he was "screened" off that job by the Coast Guard for being a "subversive."

"A fellow named John Mahoney up in Seattle had been fired for criticizing the bureaucracy of the union," Halstead recalled.

"A lot of people who had come to his defense were fired. I had passed out some leaflets on the case. That's probably the reason my name got turned over to the Coast Guard."

After going to school on the GI Bill for a while, Halstead got a job as an automobile worker and became active in a United Auto Workers (UAW) organizing drive.

"The Korean War came along and we lost that drive, in part because of the hysteria around the war and the red-baiting that developed."

Halstead next learned garment cutting, which has been his trade ever since. As a member of the International Ladies' Garment Workers' Union (ILGWU), he participated in the union's organizing campaigns. At times, Halstead was assigned by the union to get a job in an unorganized shop. The ILGWU paid him the difference between the salary he received there and union-scale wages, while he spearheaded the drive for union recognition.

Halstead also participated in efforts during that period to organize agricultural workers in California.

In 1953 Halstead moved to Detroit, where he landed a job in an automobile plant cutting cloth for the upholstery in cars.

"I had been working there for about a year when the Square D strike broke out," Halstead said. That strike occurred during the depths of the witch-hunt and was of some importance.

Square D was an electrical manufacturing firm under contract to the United Electrical Workers, which was one of the unions expelled from the CIO for "Communist domination." The company was out to break the strike and was nearly successful.

What finally saved the union was the massive response of UAW militants, including Fred Halstead, who rallied to the defense of the Square D strikers and beat back the company and the scab-herding cops. In the course of the strike, Halstead became the victim of a frame-up attempt by the Detroit police and their "loyalty" squad. But the cops' red-scare hoax failed, and the charges were eventually dropped.

When the movement against United States involvement in Vietnam began to develop, Halstead became one of its leaders. He joined the staff of the New York Fifth Avenue Vietnam Peace Parade Committee upon its inception in 1965, and he remained there until he left to run for president in 1967. After his campaign, he again worked in the antiwar movement, and he was involved in organizing every major national demonstration.

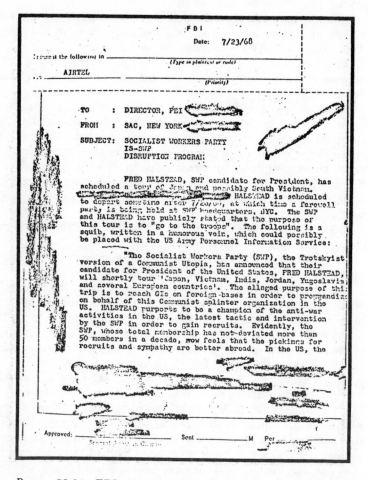

F B I

Date: 7/23/68

Transmit the following in _____
                              (Type in plaintext or code)

AIRTEL
                              (Priority)

TO   :   DIRECTOR, FBI

FROM   :   SAC, NEW YORK

SUBJECT: SOCIALIST WORKERS PARTY
            IS-SWP
            DISRUPTION PROGRAM

FRED HALSTEAD, SWP candidate for President, has
scheduled a tour of Japan and possibly South Vietnam.
HALSTEAD is scheduled
to depart sometime after 7/29/68, at which time a farewell
party is being held at SWP headquarters, NYC. The SWP
and HALSTEAD have publicly stated that the purpose of
this tour is to "go to the troops". The following is a
squib, written in a humorous vein, which could possibly
be placed with the US Army Personnel Information Service:

"The Socialist Workers Party (SWP), the Trotskyist
version of a Communist Utopia, has announced that their
candidate for President of the United States, FRED HALSTEAD,
will shortly tour 'Japan, Vietnam, India, Jordan, Yugoslavia,
and several European countries'. The alleged purpose of this
trip is to reach GIs on foreign bases in order to propagandize
on behalf of this Communist splinter organization in the
US. HALSTEAD purports to be a champion of the anti-war
activities in the US, the latest tactic and intervention
by the SWP in order to gain recruits. Evidently, the
SWP, whose total membership has not deviated more than
50 members in a decade, now feels that the pickings for
recruits and sympathy are better abroad. In the US, the

Approved: _____ Sent _____ M Per _____

Pages 58-61: *FBI memos proposing to disrupt Fred Hal
stead's 1968 visit to Vietnam to talk to GIs. The tactic is the
familiar one of planting red-baiting information in the
press—in this case the armed forces press, using military*

58

"SWP has recently suffered its usual reversal among fellow radical organizations in its attempts to infiltrate and dominate the anti-war scene. HALSTEAD is scheduled to push for the return of all US personnel abroad. As a past champion of FIDEL CASTRO, he believes all countries should be left to fend for themselves and establish their future Utopias on the scale of the current Cuban Paradise. Intervention into the affairs of nations by countries or forces other than "the imperialist US" is not a plank in HALSTEAD's platform. It should be an interesting experience for Mr. HALSTEAD when he encounters the men who have served both their own country and others in the interest of freedom".

- 2 -

intelligence channels. This operation had one additional special feature: the FBI "news" item ends with a thinly veiled invitation to GIs to assault the antiwar leader.

UNITED STATES GOVERNMENT

Memorandum

TO :

FROM :

DATE: July 25, 1968

SUBJECT: SOCIALIST WORKERS PARTY
DISRUPTION PROGRAM
INTERNAL SECURITY - SWP

PURPOSE:

This memorandum recommends we furnish a blind memorandum to the intelligence branches of the Armed Forces by Liaison which would hamper the efforts of the leader of the Socialist Workers Party in trying to contact members of the Armed Forces abroad.

BACKGROUND:

Fred Halstead, Socialist Workers Party (SWP) candidate for President of the United States, has scheduled a tour of various foreign countries to "go to the troops." The SWP is a communist splinter group designated under Executive Order 10450 which has been active in campus unrest, anti-Vietnam protests, antidraft and racial demonstrations. Information concerning his trip has been previously disseminated.

New York has prepared a squib which describes Halstead and the SWP in an uncomplimentary manner. New York recommended the squib be furnished the Army for use in its publications to decrease the effectiveness of Halstead's efforts to contact military personnel. We believe the squib should be furnished the intelligence branches of all the services through Liaison in order to get the maximum benefit for use in the publications of the Armed Forces.

CONTINUED - OVER

60

Memorandum to [redacted]
Re: Socialist Workers Party
    Disruption Program

        The proposed squib is attached in blind memorandum form. It does not jeopardize any sources.

RECOMMENDATION:

        It is recommended the squib be approved and sent by Liaison to the intelligence branches of the Armed Forces.

Today, after years of antiwar demonstrations by veterans and frequent manifestations of antiwar sentiment within the military, it may seem hard to believe that at first many opponents of the war wrote off GIs as "war criminals" and rejected the possibility of winning them as allies. But that was all too frequently the case.

"When the antiwar movement came along, there were discussions about where we should spread the word," Halstead recalled. "One obvious place, I would suggest, was right inside the army.

" 'You're crazy,' people would say to me. 'They are butchers, and there is nothing we can do about that.'

"I would tell them that they were wrong, that GIs are just ordinary people who will be responsive to the same arguments as civilians," Halstead continued.

"I knew GIs could be reached because I had been a GI myself and I had seen GIs organize."

The Trip to Vietnam

Why did Halstead decide to visit Vietnam in the summer of 1968? During the presidential campaign that year Lyndon Johnson tried to convey the impression that the war was almost over. Nixon and Humphrey, the candidates of the two capitalist parties, made a pact between themselves not to make the war an issue in the campaign.

The SWP's candidate went to Vietnam as part of the socialist strategy to try to inject the war into the presidential campaign as *the* major issue.

"We demanded the immediate withdrawal of the American forces as the only way to end the killing over there and as the only legal and moral thing for the United States to do," Halstead recalled.

"That year there was a tendency on the part of some in the antiwar movement to get into electoral activity as a *substitute* for antiwar demonstrations. Through this campaign we encouraged the antiwar movement to stay in the streets."

There was another reason for making the trip. "We wanted to illustrate to the antiwar movement that it could reach GIs," Halstead said, "and we wanted to demonstrate to the GIs that the antiwar movement was on their side."

On August 15, 1968, Fred Halstead arrived in Saigon. He was accompanied by Barry Sheppard, who was at that time editor of the *Militant*. They spent five days in Vietnam, including a visit to the big army base at Long Binh, talking with GIs. The *Militant* carried reports from Vietnam on what they found.

"We were interested in talking to the American GIs who were on the scene," Halstead said. "They had a right to vote and to listen to what the candidates had to say. They also had a right to have an opinion on the war—a greater right than any American citizen, including the president. I went there to ask them what that opinion was."

What did he find? "The overwhelming majority of them were not willing to suddenly join the peace movement, but they weren't supporters of the war either," Halstead remembered.

They were mainly confused, looking for answers, still making up their minds. "That was all the more reason for the antiwar movement to have the stance and attitude that they were interested in reaching GIs—were on their side," Halstead observed.

I also asked Barry Sheppard about his impressions. "We found no hostility to us among any troops," he recalled, "including those who were for the war at that point."

"There were some antiwar figures who thought I would get into trouble talking to GIs in Vietnam," Halstead remembered. "And I might have gotten into some difficulty speaking to the GIs the way they did. If I had called them butchers and told them they were immoral for not refusing the draft, I probably would have gotten a fist in my face."

Instead, Halstead explained that he was a candidate from the United States who was active in the antiwar movement. He said that he thought this country never belonged in Vietnam and should get out immediately.

"I was received in a courteous and sometimes friendly way," Halstead remembered. "Never in a hostile way."

Is there any evidence that the FBI was successful in its goal of getting their story about Halstead into the military press in order to provoke an attack? The item was never picked up and printed as far as Halstead knows.

"The response we found among the soldiers in Vietnam is the key to understanding why this particular project failed," Sheppard observed. "Even those who supported the war offered no strong political motivation. They would argue along the lines that since so many lives had already been lost, the war should continue so that those deaths would not have been in vain. An appeal to anticommunism wasn't put forward as a compelling reason to stay in Vietnam."

However, Sheppard and Halstead both remembered something, which in retrospect they feel might have been a setup under FBI influence. The incident was reported in the *Militant* at the time.

Among the best places to meet and talk with GIs, they found, were the bars. One day the two socialists were sitting on stools at a bar, when a white sailor sat down beside Sheppard and began talking. While Fred was carrying on a conversation with a group of Black GIs on the other side, the white sailor made a remark about "Black power niggers." It was clearly audible to the Black soldiers.

A Black GI immediately reached over and smashed the sailor in the face. There rapidly ensued a fist fight, which Halstead and Sheppard managed to avoid. Fortunately, the automatic rifles which some of the GIs in the bar were carrying did not come into play.

Halstead and Sheppard suspect that the white sailor could have been acting under instructions to start a fight in hopes that the two socialists would become caught up—or even seriously injured—in a fight between Black and white GIs. On the other hand, they think it could have been, as Halstead put it, "just a little piece of America."

The antiwar movement as a whole would soon be convinced of the possibility of reaching GIs. "What really changed their mind was that they saw with their own eyes the GIs turning against the war," Halstead told me. "You couldn't draft 30,000 youth a month in 1968 and 1969 without getting a lot who had been involved in the antiwar movement in one way or another. Then it just spread all over the army."

The interview with Halstead took place in April 1975. The Saigon army was collapsing and the revolutionary forces were sweeping through Vietnam. By drastically limiting Washington's ability to use its military forces in China, the movement Halstead had seen almost thirty years before when he was a GI in the Pacific had been instrumental in the victory of the Chinese Revolution.

Did he see any parallels with Vietnam? "I think the fact that the United States finds it so difficult to put its military forces back into Vietnam is a very important factor in the victories that the liberation forces have won.

"The Pentagon keeps moaning that their hands are tied. Well, what tied their hands is the American antiwar movement."

3 Targeting a Black candidate: 'Determine if there is anything derogatory in his background'

"A review is being conducted of CLIFTON DE BERRY's file to determine if there is anything derogatory in his background which might cause embarrassment to the SWP if publicly exposed."

Those words appear in a secret FBI memorandum dated October 17, 1963. Of the nearly 1,000 pages of Cointelpro files released in response to the SWP suit, more concern Clifton DeBerry than any other single individual. In 1964 DeBerry became the first Black person ever to run for president of the United States, when he was nominated by the SWP.

Why was the FBI so interested in DeBerry? What was it about this man and his political activities that caused the FBI to devote so much energy to trying to discredit him?

To find the answer to these questions, the *Militant* talked with DeBerry about his background—his many years of activity in the union movement and the Black liberation struggle.

DeBerry was born in Holly Springs, Mississippi. His family sent him at a young age to live with relatives in Chicago, where they hoped he would find more opportunities open to him.

Instinctively a rebel, DeBerry was becoming involved in "the gang-war scene and about to get into trouble." Fortunately, he ran into a friend who persuaded him to go down South and take part in some union organizing efforts.

In late 1942 the two went to Louisiana, where they organized textile workers. "Then we went to a little town just outside Nashville [Tennessee] and organized a John Deere farm equipment plant there," DeBerry recalled.

After returning to Chicago and participating in several

different union organizing drives, DeBerry landed a job at the big International Harvester plant.

"They started me off in the shipping department at seventy-seven cents an hour. Our job classification was 'laborer,'" DeBerry remembered. "I had a talk with the grievance committee representative about changing the wording. We organized the guys and went out on strike for a couple of hours after lunch."

They won. Along with the classification change came a pay boost up to $1.35 an hour. "After that the guys there wanted to make me shop steward. But they already had one—an old-timer, who I later learned was in the Communist party.

"But since the workers were determined to make me their shop steward, some people from the CP contacted me. They told me I had to join the CP to become a shop steward. That's how I came to join the Communist party."

After the war, a strike wave swept the country. The FBI's investigation of DeBerry's background discovered that "labor trouble" charges were placed on his record during this period. How did this happen?

"We were organized at this time by a very dynamic leader, who later became president of the local. He saw the strikes coming and inspired a lot of us young guys to get prepared.

"We all went out to an old automobile junk yard. There we practiced until we had developed a technique for 'dumping' cars. That means turning them over. In anticipation of possible attempts by scabs to cross the picket lines in their cars, we constituted roving picket squads of five or six each."

The American working class was in a combative mood. They won some healthy wage increases from the corporations, which were obviously in a position to grant them because of their huge war profits.

DeBerry soon became well known to the Chicago police "labor squad." They developed the habit of picking up DeBerry and his friends as soon as they appeared on the scene of a strike. The cops would take them to the station but would soon release them without pressing charges, thus effectively preventing them from performing their scab-removal operation. "That is the reason so little shows up on my record," DeBerry commented.

As always during a workers' upsurge, the creativity and ingenuity of the rank and file came to the fore, and DeBerry gave an example.

"There was this group of three women who also traveled from

picket line to picket line. They had devised a method of disabling scab drivers by throwing an air-raid warden's helmet at the windshield of the car. The driver would instinctively throw his hands up to protect his face. At that point we would move in and dump the car.

"One day a big battle was shaping up at Jones Foundry. My squad showed up early in the morning. Right away we got picked up by the cops and taken downtown. They soon released us, and we headed straight back to Jones.

"We met up with those three women and were getting ready to dump some cars, when the cops nabbed us all. They threw us into the back of one of those big, square-back paddy wagons and proceeded to take us to the station.

"Now, these women had been arrested so many times that they had developed this special trick. They would station one person at the front of the wagon to look through a tiny peephole in order to see where the vehicle was headed.

"As the cops began to steer into a left turn, the one at the peephole would signal to the others—who were sitting on benches on either side of the wagon—to prepare to stand up and move to the right. If they did this during the turn, it would flip the paddy wagon over. Another person stationed by the door would kick it just as the vehicle hit the ground. This would automatically knock the doors open, so the passengers could escape.

"So, we followed their instructions. It worked, and we headed straight back to the picket line.

"Of course, they came looking for us. They picked us up again, took us back downtown, and booked us this time," DeBerry said. "That explains how I got those charges on my record."

The Cold War

In the late 1940s the cold war began to grow more intense. The United States rulers' international offensive against the Soviet Union was accompanied by a domestic offensive against the labor movement, as well as against the American CP. The trade-union bureaucracy capitulated to the ruling class on both fronts.

At first the leadership of the Congress of Industrial Organizations had hesitated to endorse the new cold war foreign policy. But during the presidential elections of 1948 they backed Truman, and along with this endorsement came support of Truman's cold war policies. This was codified at the 1948 CIO convention.

The CP followed a smaller wing of the ruling class, represented by Henry Wallace and his Progressive party, which preferred a kind of détente with the Soviet Union—a continuation of the wartime cooperation.

The cutting edge of the attack on the labor movement was the Taft-Hartley Act, which had been enacted in 1947. The labor movement refused to take up a serious fight against it. Among the provisions of the new law was a prohibition on members of the CP holding office in trade unions.

"The heads of a few of the unions, including mine [the Farm Equipment Workers], were known Stalinists," DeBerry said. "Philip Murray, the president of the CIO, handed them an ultimatum that they had to get rid of these CP union officials, in accordance with the provisions of Taft-Hartley, or leave the CIO."

It was at this time that DeBerry began to run into problems with the CP. Along with the president of his local, DeBerry was among those union militants who felt that the Stalinist officials were placing their own personal posts above the interests of a unified labor movement.

At the 1949 convention the CP-led unions were expelled from the CIO.

Around this time the Farm Equipment Workers merged with the United Electrical Workers, another Stalinist-controlled union. "After that, the CP took over almost everything in my local," DeBerry remembered.

"I had differences with them on a number of questions, including some of their policies during the Second World War— the no-strike pledge, civil rights, and Black caucuses."

The economic boom during the war brought unprecedented numbers of Blacks into the plants. In some factories, where they were assigned the hardest and most dangerous work, Blacks constituted a large percentage of the workers. A Black caucus movement began to emerge.

"I would discuss this caucus idea with some of the stewards in my shop and with Black leaders I knew in other locals. We decided it was a good and necessary idea in order to fight the special oppression of Blacks," DeBerry recalled.

The Black caucus movement led to the formation of the National Negro Labor Council at a convention in Cincinnati in 1950. "I was a delegate from my local. The CP was very instrumental in setting up the whole thing, but they were actually opposed to the formation of Black caucuses, although they were reluctant to come out and say it."

It was at that convention that Jean Tussey, an SWP member, sold a friend of DeBerry's a copy of the *Militant*. They liked what they read and asked if there was a chapter of the SWP in Chicago. "She said there was and gave us the names of some people to look up."

DeBerry was approaching an important turning point in his life. He would soon join the SWP. In 1964 he would be the party's candidate for president of the United States and would become a prime target of the FBI.

As DeBerry moved closer to the SWP and began to raise political questions with the Stalinist leadership of the Communist party, the pressure on him mounted. The CP began to bring in "specialists" who tried to persuade DeBerry politically of the error of his ways. When that failed, the CP tried other methods.

"I ran into a couple of dudes from the neighborhood hanging around the gates in front of the plant," DeBerry recalled. "I happened to ask them what they were up to, and they told me they were there to 'educate' somebody. After a little probing I discovered they were being paid to 'educate' me.

"I convinced them that they should collect the money from the people who had put them up to this but there was no need to do the job."

Not long after this, things came to a head. There was an impending strike, which the CP was desperately trying to avert. The stewards' body voted to go out, and since the CP-controlled leadership had made no provisions for a strike, the stewards were forced to assume organizational responsibility.

But the combination of a demoralizing scandal over the CP's misuse of union funds, a House Un-American Activities Committee visit to Chicago to red-bait the union, and a well-organized strikebreaking effort led to the defeat of the strike.

"After we went back I was fired," DeBerry said. "I've always thought the CP and the company got together to get rid of me, partly because other CP members on the executive board were retained."

The country was in the grip of the McCarthyite witch-hunt, and years before the incidents documented in the Cointelpro papers, DeBerry became familiar with the way the FBI operates. "I would get a job, and it would only last three days. I would go from one

UNITED STATES GOVERNMENT

Memorandum

Director, FBI ⎡⎯⎯⎯⎯⎯⎤   DATE: 10/17/63

SAC, New York ⎡⎯⎯⎯⎯⎯⎯⎯⎯⎯⎤

SOCIALIST WORKERS PARTY
IS-SWP
DISRUPTION PROGRAM

ReBulet, 10/3/63.

On 10/14/63, the anonymous letter authorized in relet was prepared on a manual typewriter utilizing commercially purchased stationery. The letter was mailed 10/14/63 from a suburb of NYC.

The Bureau will be advised if any tangible results are noted from this disruptive tactic.

The NY Local of the SWP is presently running a candidate for the position of Councilman-at-large in the borough of Brooklyn. A review is being conducted of CLIFTON DE BERRY's file to determine if there is anything derogatory in his background which might cause embarassment to the SWP if publicly exposed. It is noted that on a previous occasion it was possible to have printed in a daily NY newspaper the prison record of an SWP election candidate.

If a review of DE BERRY's file reflects a disruptive move is feasible, the Bureau will be advised.

While he was still running for city council in Brooklyn, the FBI's New York office targeted Clifton DeBerry for its favorite tactic against Black candidates—try to dredge up a prison or arrest record and get it sensationalized in the press.

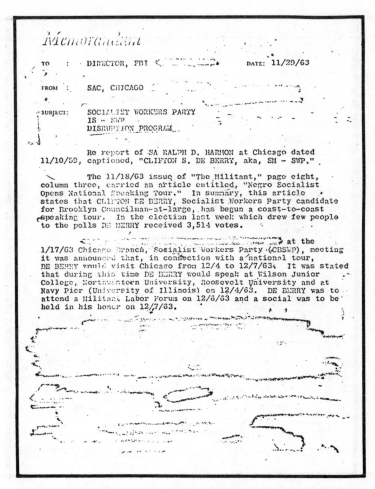

Memorandum

TO : DIRECTOR, FBI DATE: 11/29/63

FROM : SAC, CHICAGO

SUBJECT: SOCIALIST WORKERS PARTY
IS - SWP
DISRUPTION PROGRAM

Re report of SA RALPH D. HARMON at Chicago dated
11/10/59, captioned, "CLIFTON S. DE BERRY, aka, SM - SWP."

The 11/18/63 issue of "The Militant," page eight,
column three, carried an article entitled, "Negro Socialist
Opens National Speaking Tour." In summary, this article
states that CLIFTON DE BERRY, Socialist Workers Party candidate
for Brooklyn Councilman-at-large, has begun a coast-to-coast
speaking tour. In the election last week which drew few people
to the polls DE BERRY received 3,514 votes.

at the
1/17/63 Chicago Branch, Socialist Workers Party (CBSWP), meeting
it was announced that, in connection with a national tour,
DE BERRY would visit Chicago from 12/4 to 12/7/63. It was stated
that during this time DE BERRY would speak at Wilson Junior
College, Northwestern University, Roosevelt University and at
Navy Pier (University of Illinois) on 12/4/63. DE BERRY was to
attend a Militant Labor Forum on 12/6/63 and a social was to be
held in his honor on 12/7/63.

*The bureau kept close track of DeBerry's activities. One
reason is given in this memo: he received 3,500 votes in a
local election despite low voter turnout—quite a showing for
a socialist in 1964. As the accompanying essay explains,
FBI interest in DeBerry dated from his days as a labor
organizer.*

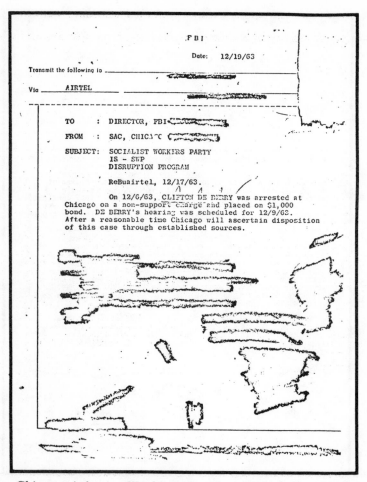

FBI

Date: 12/19/63

Transmit the following in _____

Via ___ AIRTEL ___

TO : DIRECTOR, FBI

FROM : SAC, CHICAGO

SUBJECT: SOCIALIST WORKERS PARTY
IS - SWP
DISRUPTION PROGRAM

ReBuairtel, 12/17/63.

On 12/6/63, CLIFTON DE BERRY was arrested at Chicago on a non-support charge and placed on $1,000 bond. DE BERRY's hearing was scheduled for 12/9/63. After a reasonable time Chicago will ascertain disposition of this case through established sources.

Chicago informs Washington that DeBerry has been arrested on nonsupport charges—just the sort of "derogatory information" the bureau was looking for in the memo on page 70. Several pages of the memo on page 71 were censored; these pages may have outlined a plan to engineer the Chicago arrest.

SAC, New York   9/14/64

Director, FBI

SOCIALIST WORKERS PARTY
INTERNAL SECURITY-SWP
DISRUPTION PROGRAM

Reurlet August 24, 1964.

The Bureau has realerted its contacts relative to the derogatory information concerning Clifton DeBerry. The Bureau, of course, cannot insist that such material be used; however, it is possible that through this additional contact the information may subsequently be used. You should consequently advise the Bureau of any information concerning the use of the material.

NOTE:

In April, 1964, the New York Office recommended and the Bureau approved the release to certain public sources information of a derogatory nature concerning Clifton DeBerry. DeBerry is a functionary of the SWP and is its candidate for President of the United States in 1964. The derogatory information referred to past arrests of DeBerry on nonsupport charges of his wife and children and also information relative to his living with the daughter of the National Secretary of the SWP.

The Crime Records Division released this information to a press source, however, there is no indication it has ever been used. Crime Records Division has advised that it has realerted its contact to the DeBerry material and it is hoped something will now be done with it.

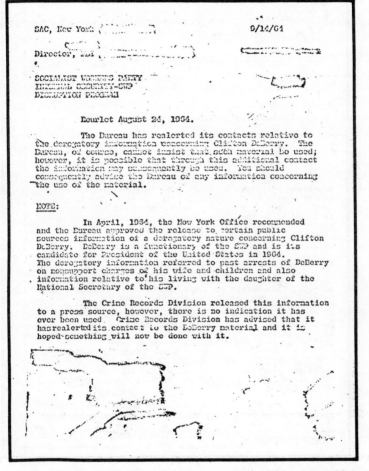

Pages 73-77: The FBI appears to become increasingly exasperated as months go by and the media fail to publicize DeBerry's arrest, despite repeated bureau efforts to contrive a scandal over his personal life.

UNITED STATES GOVERNMENT

Memorandum

DIRECTOR, FBI ⌇⌇⌇⌇⌇⌇⌇⌇⌇   DATE: 4/22/65

SAC, NEW YORK ⌇⌇⌇⌇⌇⌇⌇⌇

SOCIALIST WORKERS PARTY
IS-SWP
DISRUPTION PROGRAM
(OO: NY)

ReNYlet, 3/25/64.

Referenced letter set forth a disruptive tactic involving   CLIFTON DE BERRY, who in 1964, was campaigning as SWP candidate for President of the US.   The tactic involved release of public source material identifying DE BERRY as having a police record, deserting one wife and living adulterously with another, the daughter of FARRELL DOBBS, National Secretary of the SWP.

It is felt that public knowledge of the above would reflect adversely upon the SWP.

The Bureau approved the idea and furnished the material to a Bureau contact. The information never was printed, however, as far as the NYO knows.

The SWP weekly newspaper, "The Militant" announced in its 3/22/65, issue that CLIFTON DE BERRY had been nominated as SWP candidate for mayor of NYC in the 1965 elections. He said he intended to start his campaign early.

DE BERRY will attempt to utilize public platforms, radio and television to spread SWP propaganda, and the disruptive tactic proposed in relet is again regarded as having a good potential.

The Bureau is requested to approve again the release of the derogatory information regarding DE BERRY.

If circumstances relating to the Bureau contact preclude his using the material, the NYO will submit its recommendations regarding using this data in an anonymous mailing.

-2-

SAC, New York ⟨⟩   5/7/65

Director, FBI

SOCIALIST WORKERS PARTY
INTERNAL SECURITY - SWP
DISRUPTION PROGRAM

    Reference is made to New York letters dated 4/22/65 and
3/25/64, and Bureau letter to New York dated 9/14/64.

    On two occasions the derogatory information concerning
Clifton DeBerry has been brought to the attention of Bureau
contacts. However, these contacts have not seen fit to use the
information. Therefore, no further effort will be made to obtain
a release of this information through these contacts.

    New York is requested to submit a recommendation regarding
the use of this derogatory material in an anonymous letter as set
forth in referenced New York letter of 4/22/65.

NOTE:

    On two occasions derogatory information concerning Clifton
DeBerry was furnished to Bureau contacts for possible use in newspapers to discredit DeBerry's campaign for the President of the
United States in 1964 on the Socialist Workers Party ticket. DeBerry
is now running for the position of mayor of New York City. New York
has suggested this derogatory material be again brought to the
attention of Bureau contacts. Inasmuch as this material was not
utilized by Bureau contacts on two previous occasions, no effort
is being made to again bring the information to the attention of
these contacts.

UNITED STATES GOVERNMENT

Memorandum

DIRECTOR, FBI   DATE: 10/29/65

SAC, NEW YORK

SOCIALIST WORKERS PARTY
IS-SWP
DISRUPTION PROGRAM

ReBulet to NY, 6/21/65.

    Relet set forth that action would be initiated at
the Seat of Government re dissemination of derogatory background
concerning CLIFTON DE BERRY, SWP Candidate for Mayor of NYC.

    DE BERRY has made several public speeches, radio
and television appearances, but the NYO has noted no questioning
of him tending to bring out his background. Similarly, there
has been no critical comment re DE BERRY in this connection in
the press.

    Since the NYC elections will be held 11/2/65, it
appears that no positive results have been obtained from
this operation.

77

job to another, and it would be the same story. The FBI would visit my boss, and I would be fired."

DeBerry finally managed to hang on to a job when a stubborn employer refused to fire him. Nonetheless, he was told that FBI agents continued to come around every three or four days to "check up" on him. DeBerry eventually got into painting, and he remains a painter by trade.

The Civil Rights Movement

In 1954 the U.S. Supreme Court handed down its historic decision on school desegregation. Soon the country would witness a new Black civil rights movement and the opening stages of a new radicalization. At this time the center of DeBerry's political activity shifted from the trade-union movement to another arena of the class struggle.

DeBerry was active in the Chicago chapter of the NAACP and in the Washington Park Forum, a Black community organization. In 1955, news of the lynching of Emmett Till, a Black youth from Chicago, jolted the Black community. Till was murdered by racists while visiting relatives in Mississippi. DeBerry was instrumental in organizing a mass meeting to protest the lynching.

The 1955–56 Montgomery, Alabama, bus boycott to end segregation on the buses signaled the beginning of the civil rights movement. In Chicago, DeBerry organized a Station Wagons to Montgomery Committee, which raised funds to purchase vehicles for use by boycotters.

DeBerry personally delivered one of the station wagons to Montgomery, where he stayed at the home of E.D. Nixon. Like DeBerry, Nixon was a veteran of the union movement who brought his organizational and political know-how to the new Black civil rights struggle. Nixon was actually the central organizer of the boycott.

"I talked with Nixon about the boycott movement, how it originated, how it functioned, and what they expected to gain," DeBerry recalled. "For the first time I met Dr. Martin Luther King, who had been persuaded to enter the fight by Nixon."

In 1960 DeBerry moved to New York. That same year a sit-in movement to desegregate public accommodations began in the South. Supporters of the desegregation fight organized a boycott of the Woolworth chain in cities outside the South in a successful attempt to bring added pressure to end segregation. DeBerry threw himself into building the Woolworth boycott in Brooklyn.

In the early 1960s a Black nationalist mood was becoming visible in the ghettos of the North, and no one better articulated this new consciousness than Malcolm X.

"We began to make contact with Malcolm when he was still the main spokesman for the Nation of Islam," DeBerry said. "In late 1963 I went on a speaking tour. Malcolm was touring at the same time, and I would go to see him whenever I could."

It was during a tour stop in Chicago that the FBI arranged to have DeBerry arrested in order to create a scandal they hoped to use to discredit him. Just as DeBerry was about to address a socialist meeting, the Chicago police stormed into the building, hauled him to the station, and booked him on charges of nonsupport of his ex-wife.

There are many censored passages throughout the Cointelpro papers, but there are *entire pages* concerning this operation that were totally blank when they were turned over to the SWP by the FBI. These blank pages obviously detailed the maneuvers the FBI engaged in to engineer DeBerry's arrest.

The FBI followed up this arrest by devoting enormous attention to trying to get the news media to report both this incident and DeBerry's earlier arrests for "labor trouble."

The 1964 Campaign

On January 7, 1964, the National Committee of the Socialist Workers party announced the nomination of DeBerry as the SWP's candidate for president.

Lyndon Johnson was running for reelection, and he was opposed by Barry Goldwater. Johnson campaigned as a "peace candidate" who was opposed to escalating the war, while Goldwater favored increased bombing. Most Americans took Johnson's peace rhetoric for good coin, and he won a landslide victory.

Virtually the entire left supported Johnson's candidacy. Among the most enthusiastic backers of the Democratic candidate were the members of the CP, whose attitude was summed up in the title of a pamphlet by Gus Hall: *The Eleventh Hour—Defeat The New Fascist Threat!*

The SWP, in contrast, clearly nailed Johnson as the imperialist warrior he was. The historical record now shows how right the SWP was.

In August 1964, a supposed Vietnamese attack on U.S. ships off the coast of North Vietnam provided the excuse for rushing a special resolution through Congress. It was under the authority of this Gulf of Tonkin resolution that Johnson and the subsequent presidents committed the United States to a massive military intervention in Vietnam.

DeBerry charged that the whole thing had been set up by the White House and the Pentagon. "The incidents between the U.S. destroyer and the PT boats were the pretext, not the cause, of the U.S. air attack," DeBerry said at the time. Several years later the Pentagon papers would prove that he was totally correct.

"We of the Socialist Workers party say get all the U.S. troops, planes, and warships out of Vietnam—North and South," DeBerry demanded. "If as Johnson claims their purpose is to 'protect democracy,' then send them to Mississippi and let them do some protecting of Black Americans there."

While the FBI was secretly plotting against the Black presidential candidate, he was publicly blasting the FBI. After the disappearance of three civil rights workers slain by racists in Mississippi, DeBerry exposed the bureau's complicity.

Local cops, who were involved in the murders, had held the three in jail before they were killed. "While the three kidnapped youths were in jail in Philadelphia, Mississippi, their co-workers became fearful for their safety, and telephoned the FBI in Jackson. The FBI agent . . . refused to help and told the rights fighters that he wouldn't have any more dealings with them," DeBerry said.

In July 1964 a group of major civil rights leaders, including Roy Wilkins and Martin Luther King, issued a call for a "moratorium" on civil rights demonstrations until after election day. The purpose was to make it easier for Johnson to hold on to the racist vote, which was threatening to go to Goldwater.

DeBerry condemned the move: "This is the surest way for Negroes to get nothing. . . . Black people must develop independent political force. That's the only way they can be a power and the only way they can defend themselves against the attacks of the racists which will come whether Johnson or Goldwater is elected."

When Malcolm X, who was in Egypt at the time, heard about the moratorium, he had a similar reaction. The Black leaders "have sold themselves out and become campaign managers in the Negro community for Lyndon Johnson," he charged.

During this period DeBerry's relationship with Malcolm continued to develop. "After his break with the Nation of Islam, I used to meet with him almost every Saturday when he was in the country. We would have discussions about politics—often comparing notes and checking up on what each other had been hearing about the developing nationalist response among Blacks," DeBerry recalled.

At the suggestion of Malcolm and his collaborator, James Shabazz, DeBerry spoke at a couple of classes at the Muslim Mosque, Inc., which Malcolm headed.

"We were again touring at the same time, and our paths would often criss-cross. Whenever I could I would attend his speeches. While he was too busy to make it to mine, he would send someone over," DeBerry remembered. "We had that kind of relationship."

A few months later Malcolm would be assassinated. The FBI's role in that event is a story that is yet to be told.

Did DeBerry have any suspicion about the FBI's behind-the-scenes moves during his campaign? "One thing comes to mind. At the Chicago police station, when I was arrested on the nonsupport charge, I ran into a cop I knew. He had been on the labor squad during some of my earlier run-ins with the Chicago police. At one point while they were booking me, there was no one else around except the two of us. In a confidential tone he told me, 'Somebody who is high up is really interested in you.'"

4 A special hatred for Blacks

If you had picked up a copy of the *Militant* in late July 1961, you would have noticed that two of the six pages in the paper were devoted to the Socialist Workers party candidates in the upcoming New York City elections. The official trade-union movement was deep in the morass of Democratic party politics, where it remains today, and the SWP was offering the voters of New York an alternative. Four working-class candidates were running for the top positions.

The candidate for Manhattan borough president was a Black man named Clarence Franklin. "I live in a one-and-a-half-room apartment in a crowded tenement in Manhattan and I have to pay 40 percent of my total monthly wage for rent," Franklin wrote in the *Militant*. He offered a socialist solution to New York's housing problem.

At the New York FBI office there were people who pored over that issue of the *Militant* with unusual care. J. Edgar Hoover had recently sent out special instructions for FBI agents to be alert for possible Cointelpro operations, and someone in the New York office spotted the opportunity for a vicious attack against both the Black movement and the SWP.

The vast FBI arrest files told them that Clarence Franklin had some years earlier acquired a criminal record. That fact is not very unusual; many Black workers in this society find themselves in trouble with the law. But the agents in charge of Cointelpro thought they could use his record to embarrass him and the SWP and to drive a Black activist out of politics.

One of the things that come through clearest in the Cointelpro papers is that the FBI reserved a special hatred for the Black civil rights movement, and Black members of the SWP were singled out for special attention.

Cointelpro files document a pattern of systematic sabotage directed at the Black movement that makes the Watergate break-in and Donald Segretti's dirty tricks against the Democrats look like college pranks. Segretti and other Watergaters have been sent to jail, but the conspirators responsible for Cointelpro have yet to be charged with breaking any law.

Clarence Franklin was born into a family of Mississippi sharecroppers in 1932. When he was ten years old he moved to New York, where his mother went to work as a housecleaner. When he was fourteen he got a job setting pins in a bowling alley. Through the years Franklin found work as a dishwasher, porter, and construction laborer. Along the way he picked up an arrest record.

One might assume that a law enforcement agency such as the FBI would have noted with satisfaction that Franklin had not been charged with violating any law in several years and was currently engaged in perfectly legal activity—running for public office.

However, the FBI had different concerns. "Careful consideration has been given to the fact that the SWP in New York City is now getting some propaganda attention through the press, television and radio because it has succeeded in placing on the ballot four candidates for office in the New York City fall elections," the FBI wrote.

In a subsequent memorandum not printed here, the FBI elaborated. "The SWP has met with little or no opposition in carrying forth its aims and purposes and in securing positions on the ballot for its candidates. It is felt that some disruptive action should be taken. . . ."

The FBI evidently used one of its numerous agents in the news media—this one at the *Daily News*—to break the "story." The *News* published a story on Franklin's arrest record on election day. It is worth noting that the rules of fair play between Democratic and Republican politicians brand as "unfair campaign practices" eleventh-hour charges that are impossible to answer before the voters go to the polling place. This, of course, did not stop the FBI.

The FBI's evaluation of this operation shows that they were elated because Franklin became demoralized by the publicity about his past. When Franklin eventually withdrew from political activity, the FBI congratulated itself on a job well done.

Memorandum

TO : DIRECTOR, FBI

DATE: 10/20/61

FROM : SAC, NEW YORK

SUBJECT: SOCIALIST WORKERS PARTY (SWP) —
IS - SWP
DISRUPTION PROGRAM

ReBurlet to NY and other offices, dated 10/12/61.

Relet instructed NY and other offices having major SWP activity to evaluate a program aimed at disruption of the SWP and to submit views to the Bureau regarding this matter.

The NYO has given careful thought to this matter and it is felt that on a carefully selective basis, issues could be exploited which may well serve to disrupt the SWP and render it more impotent as a functioning organization.

Careful consideration has been given to the fact that the SWP in New York City is now getting some propaganda attention through the press, television and radio because it has succeeded in placing on the ballot four candidates for office in the New York City fall elections. With this background in mind, a review has been made of the candidates chosen by the SWP to represent it on the ballot and it has been found that one of them, JOHN CLARENCE FRANKLIN, appears to be particularly vulnerable in causing embarrassment to the SWP.

FRANKLIN has a criminal record which includes such offenses as larceny, burglary, drunkenness and a murder charge which was later reduced to manslaughter.

Pages 85-91: An early Cointelpro operation against a socialist candidate, which the FBI considered a model, is outlined in these documents. The victim was a former prisoner, a young Black worker who had come to see the need for social change through his own experiences. Heightened public consciousness about racism and the nature of the courts and prisons has made such smear tactics less effective in recent years.

These offenses took place during the years 1949-1956 in Albany, NY, prior to the time FRANKLIN moved to NY and became connected with the SWP. As a result, his prior criminal record is not known to the rank and file of the SWP and quite possibly is also unknown to the Party leadership.

When the SWP newspaper, "The Militant", introduced FRANKLIN as a candidate, he was described as accusing the Democrats and Republicans of dipping their hands into graft and of offering himself as an alternative to this. "The Militant" further set forth that the SWP candidates were on the side of the honest and productive people of the City and against those who insisted on enjoying privileges at other people's expense.

The SWP has consistently printed that it consistently maintained a high principled position over the years and was, contrary to other radical groups, a Party of consistent integrity.

It is felt that it is quite possible a considerable disruptive effect would result if it should become public knowledge that FRANKLIN, the candidate chosen by the SWP to represent it on the ballot, was a convicted thief and murderer. It is not believed that it would be necessary to give any large display to information of this sort, there is no doubt that a short item in the back pages of a metropolitan NY newspaper would quickly become well known within the SWP and related groups. It is believed that the effect of such a public revealment could possibly result in the following:

    1. Among the SWP membership, there could well be a feeling of disillusionment with the leadership of the Party for running such an individual as a candidate as well as distrust of FRANKLIN himself because of his past record.

2. Among the SWP's opponents in the radical field, there has always been an undercurrent of vindictive feeling and it is quite likely that the Communist Party (CP) or a rival Trotskyist group would seize upon an issue such as the FRANKLIN case to attack the principles of the SWP.

3. From the point of view from the public at large, it would seem that anyone reading an item regarding the FRANKLIN candidacy could hardly help but have a lower opinion of the SWP.

There is submitted for consideration by the Bureau a sample of the type of story which might be submitted to a friendly newspaper in this regard:

"One of the minor entries in the New York City municipal elections is the candidate of the Socialist Workers Party for Manhattan Borough President, Clarence Franklin. He was introduced in the Party's newspaper 'The Militant' in the issue of July 24 and 31, 1961, as being 'On the side of the honest productive people of the City'. Franklin accused the Democracts and Republicans of dipping their hands in graft and he offered himself as an alternative.

"In giving his background and qualifications, Franklin omitted some facts in regard to honesty and productivity which are a matter of record to the Albany Police Department. Under his full name of John Clarence Franklin, he accumulated an arrest record beginning with petit larceny in 1949, burglary and grand larceny in 1951, drunkenness in 1954 and murder in 1956.

"In especially considering its small size,
it would appear the SWP takes all honors in fielding
the candidate least well qualified for the office to
which he aspires."

There are enclosed for the Bureau a copy of
the FD 9 setting forth FRANKLIN's FBI fingerprint
record and pertinent articles printed in "The Militant"
of 7/24 and 31/61, regarding FRANKLIN.

It is recommended that the Bureau furnish the
above information to one of its contacts in the newspaper/
field. However, if this course of action is not
considered favorably in this instance, it is suggested
that the Bureau consider allowing NY to furnish the
information to a friendly newspaper in the NY area.
Should this procedure be agreeable to the Bureau, a
copy of the photograph of FRANKLIN taken by the Albany,
NY Police Department, 7/23/52, would be furnished the
newspaper contact with the suggestion that FRANKLIN
be interviewed by a reporter of the newspaper in order
that he may make his own determination that the
individual running for public office on the SWP ticket
is identical with the individual on whom the extensive
criminal record exists.

For the information of the Bureau, a new
file has been opened by the NYO on captioned case
and this office will continue to give well thought
out attention to develop all possibilities in the
future which might serve to have a disruptive effect
on the SWP.

- 4 -

SAC, New York ( )   October 30, 1961

Director, FBI ( )

SOCIALIST WORKERS PARTY
INTERNAL SECURITY - SWP
DISRUPTION PROGRAM

     Reurlet 10/20/61 captioned as above and submitting
for Bureau consideration a Disruption Program operation aimed
at causing embarrassment to the Socialist Workers Party (SWP),
its leaders and its membership.

     This suggestion is an excellent example of the type
desired by the Bureau under the Disruption Program. The Bureau
is pleased to note that the suggestion was well thought out
and it is felt that if future suggestions are submitted with
the same amount of preparation and planning, this program will
be exceedingly successful.

     The necessary action has been taken at the Bureau
to carry out your suggestion. No steps should be taken by
you concerning this operation. Should any tangible results
come to your attention as a result of Bureau-initiated action
in this matter, the Bureau should be advised promptly.

NOTE ON YELLOW:

     See cover memo ( ), same caption,
10/27/61-, TRR:cds.

89

AIRTEL

(Priority or Method of Mailing)

TO: DIRECTOR, FBI

FROM: SAC, NEW YORK

SUBJECT: SOCIALIST WORKERS PARTY
           IS-SWP
           DISRUPTION PROGRAM

ReBulet, 10/30/61.

There is enclosed copy of the column "On The Town" by CHARLES MC HARRY, which appeared on page 40 of the "New York Daily News," 11/7/61. It is noted this includes the information re JOHN CLARENCE FRANKLIN suggested by the NYO as a disruptive tactic against the SWP. Copies of the clipping are also attached in NY subject file and ████████ ████████████).

The attention of ████████ was directed to this item on 11/7/61, without, of course, revealing the Bureau as being the source. ████████ characterized this type of information as being in his opinion "dynamite," and said he believed everyone in the SWP was as ignorant as he was of FRANKLIN's background.

A membership meeting of the New York Local, SWP was held the evening of ████████, which was attended by ████████ He stated on ████████, that he had heard no mention of the newspaper story, but had noticed that JOHN CLARENCE FRANKLIN and his brothers, ROBERT and WILLIAM, also SWP members, were conspicuous by their absence. ████████ said he could not recall a meeting when one or more of the FRANKLINs were not in attendance. ████████

Approved: _____ Sent _____ M Per _____
          Special Agent in Charge

90

On the Town

By CHARLES McHARRY

His Record Speaks . . .

Civic improvement expert Victor Dallaire writes: "Charlie, how are you going to vote today?" Vic, being an independent thinker, I think I'm going to jump all over the voting machine. Bob or Looie— I'm not sure which one at this point—will get my vote for mayor. I would love to vote for LaGuardia again, but he isn't running. The one guy I have made up my mind on is John Clarence Franklin, candidate for borough president of Manhattan on the ticket of the Socialist Workers Party. John has accused his rivals of shameless dishonesty and general crookedness and has pictured himself as a public servant of utter probity. Here, if he cares to stand on it, is his record: Arrested for petty larceny in Albany in 1949; bagged for burglary and grand larceny in 1951; pulled in twice for drunkenness in 1954, and hit with a first degree murder rap, although the charge was reduced to manslaughter, in 1956. Seems he robbed a man and pushed him into the Hudson River, where his victim drowned. John was paroled from Clinton Prison in January, 1959. Although it would be interesting to see what Mr. Franklin would do as Manhattan's borough president, I think I'll vote for Mrs. Lawrence.

Anna Maria Alberghetti

Harold Minsky

* * *

Harold Minsky, currently operating in Las Vegas, will bring burlesque back to Broadway this winter. . . . George Abbott, frowning on the Twist, told Roseland's Lou Brecker, who has banned

91

Sabotaging a Civil Rights Case

The next set of documents concerns a 1964 FBI plot. The aim was to sabotage the defense of a group of civil rights workers facing prison in Monroe, North Carolina.

These FBI papers accord SWP leader George Weissman the dubious distinction of being the first publicly known subject of an FBI poem. The poet tried to frame Weissman on charges of stealing money from the Monroe home of Dr. A.E. Perry, head of the Committee to Aid the Monroe Defendants (CAMD) and vice-president of the Monroe NAACP.

The poem, along with a clipping from a North Carolina newspaper showing that Weissman had been in Perry's house at the time of a robbery, was sent to a carefully selected FBI mailing list.

In 1964 George Weissman was managing editor of the *Militant*. He had first visited Monroe in 1958 to report on the notorious "kissing case." Robert F. Williams, president of the Monroe NAACP, had received attention in the press by organizing armed defense guards, which put a stop to a series of Ku Klux Klan assaults on the Black community. The Klan focused particular attention on Dr. Perry, who had been instrumental in the struggle to integrate some of Monroe's public facilities.

In retaliation against the Black community, the local racist authorities charged two Black youths, eight and ten years old, with "assault upon a white female" for the crime of being kissed by a white playmate.

The two were tried and committed to a reformatory "possibly until they are twenty-one."

Weissman recalled these events in a recent interview.

"I was sent down for the *Militant* and wrote several stories about that case," Weissman said. Socialists aided in the formation of the Committee to Combat Racial Injustice, and Williams became its chairman.

"The committee mounted a campaign to publicize the case of these little boys and to bring pressure on the North Carolina authorities to get them released," Weissman recalled. In a matter of months, the resulting national and international protest led to their freedom.

"In this period I became personal friends with both Williams and Perry," Weissman said, "and they often visited me when they were in New York."

When a new attack on the Black community in Monroe made

the news in August 1961, members of the SWP were among the first to come to the victims' defense. This was the time of the "freedom rides." Buses filled with dedicated opponents of segregation traveled through the deep South, where they challenged laws requiring separation of the races in public accommodations.

Monroe had acquired a reputation as a Klan stronghold, and Williams invited some of the freedom riders to visit the city.

"A number of freedom riders on their return from Mississippi stopped off in Monroe to meet Williams and do what they could," Weissman remembered. "They decided to institute a week-long picket at the courthouse, the scene of many miscarriages of justice."

This enraged local racists, and after several days of picketing, things came to a head. On August 27 a mob attacked the picketers, and police responded by arresting the freedom riders.

"When word of this reached the Black community, the people became enraged and began preparing to defend themselves against a racist attack," Weissman said. "About this time a car carrying a middle-aged white couple from another city wandered into the Black community. Residents stopped the car and took its occupants to Williams's home. Williams offered to allow them to stay there until things cooled down."

The couple later left unharmed. But local authorities brought phony charges of kidnapping against Williams; Harold Reade and Richard Crowder, young Black Monroe residents; Mae Mallory, a Black woman from New York who had been working with Williams; and Robert Lowry, a white freedom rider from New York.

Williams and Mallory escaped from North Carolina, while Crowder, Reade, and Lowry were jailed in Monroe. Supporters quickly set up the CAMD to fight the anticipated extradition orders for Mallory, who was in Ohio, and Williams, whose whereabouts remained unknown, and to raise bail money for the three defendants in Monroe.

Williams soon arrived in Cuba, where he obtained asylum. The state of Ohio eventually extradited Mallory to North Carolina.

"When the case came to trial in 1964, I went down there to cover it both for the *Militant,* which gave more attention to events in Monroe than any newspaper in the country, and the *Nation* magazine," Weissman said. "I had written an article for the *Nation* at the time of the kissing case, and the editor commissioned me to do another story this time. That's how I happened to be in Monroe at the time of the robbery at Dr. Perry's home."

Perry's house served as a gathering place for supporters of the defendants during the trial.

"On this particular day, since I had to meet a *Militant* deadline, I remained in the house while the others went to court," Weissman recalled.

"While I was alone in the house, there was a phone call for Dr. Perry. When I said he was not there, the caller asked me who was there besides myself. I said there was no one.

"An hour or so later the doorbell rang, and I looked out through the glass and I saw a young Black man with an envelope. I opened the door, and he said that the envelope was for Dr. Perry. When I reached to take it, he produced a pistol."

The robber directed Weissman to the basement. A second man, whom Weissman did not see, entered the house. They tied Weissman to a chair and went upstairs.

"After they left, I freed myself," Weissman said. "About the same time Dr. Perry and the others returned from the trial. It turned out that a wall safe hidden in the closet had been broken into and robbed."

Since it was not unusual for doctors to keep money in their offices, this was assumed at the time to be a simple robbery. Weissman now has second thoughts about that.

"Looking back on it now, especially in view of the revelations about the methods of the FBI and the CIA, I wonder if they had a hand in it." There is no direct evidence of that in the Cointelpro documents currently available, but Weissman thinks it warrants looking into.

"The investigation of the robbery seemed mostly aimed at me," Weissman remembers. "The state police proposed that I take a lie detector test."

The documents on pages 95-99 outline this operation. In another document not reproduced here, the FBI openly stated that its goal was to "cause the SWP and CAMD to cease their efforts on behalf of the defendants."

The Monroe defendants' conviction was overturned, and the prosecution was not able to try the case again. However, Williams is now back in the United States and is still fighting extradition to North Carolina.

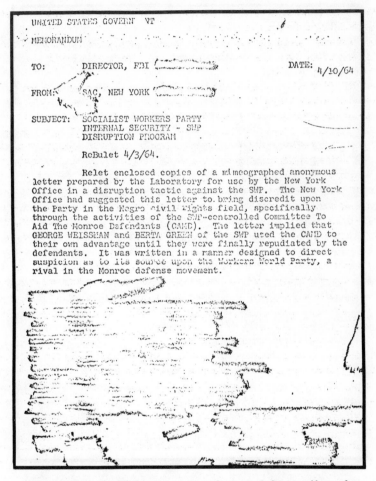

UNITED STATES GOVERN T

MEMORANDUM

TO: DIRECTOR, FBI   DATE: 4/10/64

FROM: SAC, NEW YORK

SUBJECT: SOCIALIST WORKERS PARTY
               INTERNAL SECURITY - SWP
               DISRUPTION PROGRAM

ReBulet 4/3/64.

      Relet enclosed copies of a mimeographed anonymous
letter prepared by the Laboratory for use by the New York
Office in a disruption tactic against the SWP. The New York
Office had suggested this letter to bring discredit upon
the Party in the Negro civil rights field, specifically
through the activities of the SWP-controlled Committee To
Aid The Monroe Defendants (CAMD). The letter implied that
GEORGE WEISSMAN and BERTA GREEN of the SWP used the CAMD to
their own advantage until they were finally repudiated by the
defendants. It was written in a manner designed to direct
suspicion as to its source upon the Workers World Party, a
rival in the Monroe defense movement.

*Pages 95-99: An FBI scheme to sabotage defense efforts for
framed-up Monroe civil rights activists included an anonymous letter, a newspaper clipping, and a poem. These were
sent to radical publications in an effort to create the
impression George Weissman had stolen defense committee
funds and to generate mutual suspicions within the
movement. (An earlier Monroe disruption is documented on
pages 142-148.)*

Copies of the anonymous letter were mailed on 4/8/64, in commercially purchased envelopes addressed by a clerical employee of the New York Office. The letter was sent to the individuals listed below:

(1) DANIEL WATTS
    Editor, "Liberator"
    244 East 46th Street
    New York, New York

(2) HAROLD CRUSE
    203 West 14th Street
    New York, New York

(3) Editor, "The Worker"
    23 West 26th Street
    New York, New York

(4) Editor, "National Guardian"
    197 East Fourth Street
    New York, New York

(5) JAMES BALDWIN
    470 West End Avenue
    New York, New York

(6) PETER KIHSS
    c/o New York Times
    229 West 43rd Street
    New York, New York

(7) JAMES ROBERTSON
    c/o "Spartacist"
    Box 1377, G.P.O.
    New York, New York

(8) TIM WOHLFORTH
    160 West 95th Street
    New York, New York

- 2 -

(9) LEROI JONES
     27 Cooper Square
     New York, New York

     If any information re this mailing appears in New York files designated to receive a copy of instant letter, it should be directed to subject file, so the Bureau can be advised.

     It is believed that a follow-up to this anonymous mailing may increase the effectiveness of the disruption operation. We can take advantage of the fact that GEORGE WEISSMAN reported to the Monroe police that while he was alone in the home of a Monroe Negro civil rights leader, two bandits came in and rifled a wall safe. A Xerox copy of a clipping from the Charlotte Observer of 2/27/64, outlining the story, is enclosed for information of the Bureau.

     Since recipients of the first anonymous letter are familiar with the connection of the SWP's WEISSMAN with the Monroe defense, it will not be necessary to go into a detailed exposition if they are furnished copies of the clipping. Bureau authority is requested to send a Xerox copy of the Charlotte Observer article to the same individuals named above in instant letter. Bureau is also requested to authorize enclosing with the clipping, as a device to generate further suspicions, the following bit of verse:

          Georgie-Porgie, down in Monroe,
          Found himself alone with the dough,
          Called the cops, and what did he say?
          "Bad guys came and took it away".

     If approved, Bureau is requested to have the Laboratory prepare the poem, as expeditiously as possible, ▓▓▓▓▓▓▓▓ The poem should

- 3 -

be on a mimeographed half-sheet, presumably an economy by the putative sender.

In addition to the addressees of the first anonymous letter, another will be added for the second letter, if approved by the Bureau. This is the editor of Progressive Labor, Box 808, G.P.O., Brooklyn 1, New York. This organization was also active in Monroe and as a rival of the SWP may be interested in the material to use in attacking the Party.

The Bureau is requested to advise the New York Office as soon as possible since interest in the Monroe case becomes less as time goes by.

- 4 -

Doctor's Wall Safe Cracked

N.Y. Trial Reporter Only Person Home

By DON GRAY
Observer Staff Writer

MONROE — Two bandits forced their way into the home of a Monroe Negro physician Wednesday, tied up a visitor who was the only person in the house at the time, and rifled a wall safe.

The visitor was a free - lance New York City journalist, George Weissman, who was in Monroe to cover the racial kidnap trial now going on. He said the bandits, at least one of whom had a gun, ordered him to keep quiet while they robbed the safe.

The house was owned by Dr. A. E. Perry, a former president of the Monroe NAACP chapter, who said "money" . . . just money" was taken from the safe. He said he did not know how much was taken.

"I'll have to do some figuring and I'll have to talk with my wife first," he said.

Weissman said he was at the Perry house shortly before noon when he heard someone at the door. He said a Negro man was there, asking to see Perry.

Suddenly, the man pointed a pistol at him and backed him into the house. Weissman was taken to the basement, tied up, and gagged with a piece of drapery.

A second man came into the basement then, Weissman said, but he was ordered not to turn around and look.

The two men left Weissman in the basement and went to work on the safe upstairs.

Police Lt. Ted Brome said the wall safe, hidden behind clothes in a closet, was forced open with a garden pick.

Weissman said two defense lawyers and one defendant in the kidnap trial had been living at Perry's home.

He said the lawyers and some of their clients came to the house for lunch a few minutes after the robbers left.

By that time, Weissman said, he had managed to untie himself.

"There sure is a lot going on here," Weissman said. "New York City is dull compared to Monroe."

(Indicate page, name of newspaper, city and state.)

10   CHARLOTTE OBSERVER
Charlotte, N. C.

Date: 2-27-64
Edition:
Author:
Editor:
Title:

Character:
or
Classification:

5 'Drive a wedge between the followers of Malcolm X and the SWP'

After several months of disciplinary silence imposed on him for making statements that Black Muslim leader Elijah Muhammad frowned on, Malcolm X broke discipline with remarks the whole world heard.

"Nineteen sixty-four threatens to be a very explosive year," he told a jam-packed news conference March 12, 1964, in publicly announcing his break from the Nation of Islam.

He said he was prepared to cooperate in local civil rights actions in the South and elsewhere, pointing out that every campaign for specific objectives can only heighten the political consciousness of Black people.

"We should be peaceful, law-abiding," he said, "but the time has come for the American Negro to fight back in self-defense whenever and wherever he is being unjustly and unlawfully attacked."

Then he hurled a challenge to the government:

"If the government thinks I am wrong for saying this, then let the government start doing its job."

The United States rulers, of course, did think Malcolm was wrong, and they told their FBI to start doing their job—a job they may have tried to finish on February 21, 1965, when three men gunned down Malcolm.

But their work did not stop with Malcolm's death. This is revealed in a batch of Cointelpro memos released in response to the Socialist Workers party suit to stop government surveillance and harassment.

Cointelpro was aimed at destroying socialist and Black organizations. In a 1967 letter, J. Edgar Hoover gave his reasons for initiating a special Cointelpro operation against Black organizations.

"The purpose of this new counterintelligence endeavor is to expose, disrupt, misdirect, discredit, or otherwise neutralize the activities of black nationalist, hate-type organizations and groupings, their leadership, spokesmen, membership, and supporters."

Cointelpro memos present the fuzzy outlines of the FBI's earlier attempt to blackjack relations between the SWP and the Muslim Mosque, Inc. (MMI) and the Organization of Afro-American Unity (OAAU) after Malcolm's death.

Malcolm created both organizations after his break with the Nation of Islam. The Mosque was for Muslim activists, but the OAAU did not require religious adherence for membership.

In a May 25, 1965, letter to the New York office, Hoover wrote:

"It would appear that the apparent attempt by the SWP to exploit the followers of the late Malcolm X for its own benefit offers some potential for the institution of disruptive tactics."

On June 15, 1965, New York responded: "SWP influence on the followers of MALCOLM X would be disrupted by emphasizing the atheism of the SWP as opposed to the basic religious orientation of the MMI." Washington approved.

In August 1965 the New York office wrote to Hoover boasting that the operation had soured relations between the socialists and Malcolm's followers.

"It is believed probable that the disintegrating relations between the SWP and [the OAAU] can be attributed to the disruptive tactic authorized . . . and will result in a continued loss of influence by the SWP among this group of Negroes."

In a recent interview with the *Militant,* Harlem activist Charles Kenyatta, who was prominent among Malcolm's followers, called the Cointelpro tactics "criminal," but said he was not surprised at the new revelations.

"When you have one man who was as great as Malcolm was, then you can expect these FBI and CIA tactics against him and his followers."

He said if there is anything to learn it is not to "let these petty tactics and differences divide us."

*   *   *

Although a new Cointelpro conspiracy against Black groups was launched in 1967, the documents reproduced here—and others—reveal that FBI harassment of the Black movement predates 1967.

Reflecting the U.S. rulers' fear and hatred of the Black struggle, especially militant or uncompromising organizations, the FBI and local police had singled out the Muslims for harassment and physical attacks in the early 1960s.

The *Militant* obtained a secret Los Angeles Police Department report on the Muslims and printed it in 1962.

"The men of this group are extremely dangerous," the report said, "further, they are a type of fanatic, and are willing to die for their cause, content if they can take a caucasian, preferably a police officer (and this includes Negro police officers too), with them when they are killed."

The *Militant* ran an editorial responding to the cops' racist views. "For socialists and other champions of civil rights, the question of agreement or disagreement with the Black Muslims' demands for racial separation should in no way becloud the main issue—defense of the rights of the Black Muslims against police and political persecution."

Today, virtually every voice on the left—and even many ruling-class voices—are forced to pay tribute to Malcolm. But before his death they wouldn't touch him with a ten-foot pole.

With the exception of the SWP, radical organizations had fallen victim to the false propaganda that said Malcolm thrived on white hatred and was a general, all-around troublemaker and division-monger among Black people.

This was most clearly expressed by the Communist party. In an article in the CP's August 1963 *Political Affairs,* Stalinist leader Benjamin Davis said that the civil rights demonstrations in Birmingham "dynamited the irrational and irresponsible drivel of Malcolm X and Elijah Muhammad, whose antiwhite racism, anti-Semitism and backwardness, proved utterly bankrupt. . . ."

"The pursuit of either the Muslim black-versus-white policy or the Williams' advocacy of armed insurrection cannot but be divisive of Negro unity," Davis wrote.

He was proposing, against Malcolm's and Robert F. Williams's call for Black self-defense in the face of armed racist attacks in the South, reliance on the promise of civil rights bills and handouts from white liberals.

"Opposition to the hopelessness and abject defeatism of a Malcolm X is not a matter of competing for transient applause—it is a question of principle," according to Davis.

SAC, New York _____   5/25/65

Director, FBI _____

SOCIALIST WORKERS PARTY
INTERNAL SECURITY - SWP
DISRUPTION PROGRAM

          Reference is made to New York letter dated 5/13/65
captioned, "Muslim Mosque, Inc., Internal Security - MMI."

          Referenced letter points out that the interest of the
Socialist Workers Party (SWP) in the Muslim Mosque, Inc., and
the Organization of Afro-American Unity, Inc., is obviously
self-serving. It notes that the SWP hopes to exploit the death
of Malcolm X and the feelings of his followers in an effort to
win these "militant Negroes" to the Trotskyite cause.

          It would appear that the apparent attempt by the SWP
to exploit the followers of the late Malcolm X for its own
benefit offers some potential for the institution of disruptive
tactics. You are requested to thoroughly analyze this situation
and submit comments and recommendations to the Bureau regarding
possible disruptive tactics that could be utilized against the
SWP in this connection.

NOTE:

          Referenced letter points out that a rather close
relationship has developed between the SWP and the followers
of the late Malcolm X, and the SWP hopes to recruit new
followers by this means. This situation appears to offer
some potential for the utilization of disruptive tactics against
the SWP. New York is being instructed to analyze this situation
and to submit comments and recommendations concerning possible
disruptive tactics that could be used against the SWP in this
connection.

*Pages 104-107: The FBI has not released any documents on
its operations against Malcolm X and his followers in the
period leading up to his assassination, but this bureau
correspondence dated just after his death indicates an
intense interest in the Muslim Mosque, Inc., founded by
Malcolm. The operation outlined here is occasioned by New*

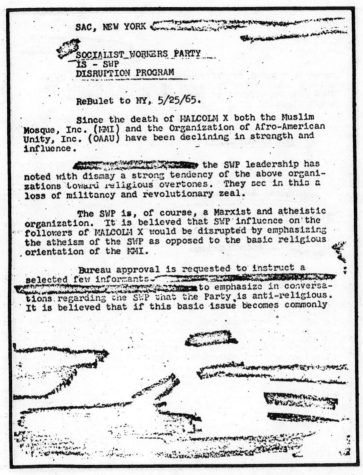

SAC, NEW YORK

SOCIALIST WORKERS PARTY
IS - SWP
DISRUPTION PROGRAM

ReBulet to NY, 5/25/65.

Since the death of MALCOLM X both the Muslim
Mosque, Inc. (MMI) and the Organization of Afro-American
Unity, Inc. (OAAU) have been declining in strength and
influence.

the SWP leadership has
noted with dismay a strong tendency of the above organizations toward religious overtones. They see in this a
loss of militancy and revolutionary zeal.

The SWP is, of course, a Marxist and atheistic
organization. It is believed that SWP influence on the
followers of MALCOLM X would be disrupted by emphasizing
the atheism of the SWP as opposed to the basic religious
orientation of the MMI.

Bureau approval is requested to instruct a
selected few informants
to emphasize in conversa-
tions regarding the SWP that the Party is anti-religious.
It is believed that if this basic issue becomes commonly

*York's alarm that "a rather close relationship has developed
between the SWP and the followers of the late Malcolm X."
The next communication notes with satisfaction that the
groups he led "have been declining in strength and
influence" since his death and proposes to use undercover
agents within the Black movement to sow discord.*

105

known as a point of difference, it would serve to drive
a wedge between the followers of MALCOLM X and the SWP,
thus foiling efforts of the Party to recruit in this
Negro field.

In conclusion, it is felt that the SWP have had some measure of success in their efforts to resolve their problems and the Muslims will present their opposition.

Nevertheless, information was developed that [illegible]

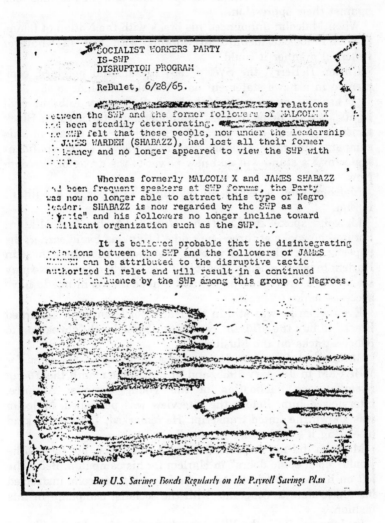

SOCIALIST WORKERS PARTY
IS-SWP
DISRUPTION PROGRAM

ReBulet, 6/28/65.

[illegible] relations between the SWP and the former followers of MALCOLM X had been steadily deteriorating. [illegible] the SWP felt that these people, now under the leadership of JAMES WARDEN (SHABAZZ), had lost all their former militancy and no longer appeared to view the SWP with favor.

Whereas formerly MALCOLM X and JAMES SHABAZZ had been frequent speakers at SWP forums, the Party was now no longer able to attract this type of Negro leader. SHABAZZ is now regarded by the SWP as a "mystic" and his followers no longer incline toward a militant organization such as the SWP.

It is believed probable that the disintegrating relations between the SWP and the followers of JAMES WARDEN can be attributed to the disruptive tactic authorized in relet and will result in a continued loss of influence by the SWP among this group of Negroes.

Buy U.S. Savings Bonds Regularly on the Payroll Savings Plan

In contrast to the CP, the SWP saw it as its responsibility to support the political actions that Malcolm and the Muslims took against their oppression.

When Malcolm announced his break with the Nation of Islam, the SWP looked forward to working with him in whatever fraternal manner it could.

Clifton DeBerry, the SWP's 1964 presidential nominee, commented in a news statement on what Malcolm had to say.

"I heartily agree with Malcolm X that every militant civil rights struggle helps the Negroes understand the need for Black political power," DeBerry said. "I will do all I can in this campaign to rally support for these views. I am confident Malcolm X's stand will add new power to the drive for Freedom Now."

Malcolm soon accepted an invitation to speak at a Militant Forum.

Malcolm spoke kindly of the *Militant*. At his first Militant Forum—he spoke at three—he said: "I think as I said earlier, the paper is one of the best I've read. We always encourage those in Harlem to buy it when we see it up there, or wherever else we may see it. It's a very good paper, and I hope they continue to have success—make progress."

Even when he was still in the Nation of Islam Malcolm urged Blacks to buy the *Militant* because of its forthright opposition to police attacks on the Muslims.

Militant staff writer Harry Ring interviewed Malcolm for WBAI-FM in January 1965, and in that same month the *Young Socialist,* the publication of the Young Socialist Alliance, interviewed him. Before the interview was published, Malcolm was shown the edited transcript. He remarked, "This is the kind of editing it's a pleasure to read."

Malcolm did not endorse DeBerry's candidacy, but he said he would "open some doors" in Harlem for his campaign. Before he left on his second trip to Africa in July 1964, Malcolm instructed his top leaders to cooperate with the socialist campaign in this fashion.

In January 1965, the YSA broached with Malcolm the idea of going on a YSA-sponsored tour of college campuses. Malcolm liked the idea but said he could not go until he returned from another scheduled trip abroad.

Malcolm opposed the Vietnam War and expressed interest in the SWP's participation in the coming April 17, 1965, antiwar march in Washington, D.C., sponsored by the Students for a Democratic Society.

All during his last year, Malcolm's views became more and more militant and anticapitalist.

The Harlem ghetto had exploded in revolt against grinding oppression in 1964, and militant nationalist beliefs—which Malcolm was best at popularizing—and Black awareness were catching on fast.

Malcolm's call for Black power was getting through to thousands of Blacks who were eager to listen.

His message also got through to a few people—including the FBI—who jerked in fear whenever they heard it.

It was a bright, spring-like Sunday when the sandy-headed Muslim minister unfolded his lanky frame behind a lectern at the Audubon Ballroom to spread his message—for the last time. From nowhere three men—who to this day have never publicly said who put them up to it—made their way to within what the coroner said was point-blank range. One pulled the triggers of the sawed-off, double-barreled shotgun he carried.

The gun, it was said, made an awesome sound.

6 'Cause disruption in the peace movement'

For over a decade, the most explosive issue in world politics was the American intervention in Vietnam. It was the growing mass opposition to the war among the American people that gave the radicalization of the sixties and seventies its biggest push.

With the American withdrawal and the fall of the Saigon dictatorship in the spring of 1975, people in all parts of the political spectrum began assessing the Vietnam War era. The revelation of the FBI's schemes against the antiwar movement provides an interesting sidelight to that review. It also helps confirm the analysis the socialists made at the beginning of the movement—that it could pose a serious threat to the power of the Pentagon and Wall Street and eventually force the government to pull out of Vietnam.

The Cointelpro papers reveal several instances of behind-the-scenes FBI maneuvers to block the development of a mass, visible protest movement against the war. A variety of techniques were employed to achieve this task.

These included promoting splits among antiwar forces, encouraging red-baiting of socialists, and pushing violent confrontations as an alternative to massive, peaceful demonstrations.

One of the more unusual operations uncovered to date is a 1966 FBI attempt to divert the Socialist Workers party from its strong commitment to the antiwar struggle.

The FBI mailed out an anonymous "Open Letter to Trotsky-ites." That and related documents are reproduced here. The letter was designed to create dissatisfaction within the party over its participation in the new movement. In particular, the FBI sought

111

to create dissension within the SWP and Young Socialist Alliance over their role at a November 1965 antiwar conference in Washington, D.C.

The mass movement against the war in Vietnam, and socialist participation in it, had begun with a call by the Students for a Democratic Society for an April 1965 March on Washington.

SDS in 1965 possessed a measure of respectability. Officially, it was still the youth group of the League for Industrial Democracy, a longtime meeting ground for conservative social democrats and union bureaucrats. Consequently, the SDS National Council's decision to call the march, made at its meeting over the December 1964 school break, carried some authority.

Doug Jenness joined the staff of the YSA national office that January. "We met with Clark Kissinger, the SDS national secretary, to discuss what we could do," he recalls. "The YSA organized three national tours—one on the West Coast, one in the Midwest, and I toured the Eastern states." YSA locals across the country quickly began to help organize student participation in the march.

During that winter, Lyndon Johnson escalated the war, and the impact helped to turn out 20,000 people, more than anyone had expected.

"The day after the march I attended an SDS National Council meeting there in Washington," Jenness said. "Surprisingly, they failed to follow up on their original initiative." SDS pulled away from the antiwar movement and never again focused its energies on a national level toward the war.

Nevertheless, the antiwar movement continued to grow. The teach-in movement, born on March 24 at the University of Michigan, spread spontaneously from campus to campus.

In late May, the Berkeley, California, Vietnam Day Committee, in which the SWP and YSA played a role, brought out 30,000 people for a thirty-four-hour marathon teach-in and protest against the war.

Meeting in Washington, D.C., August 6-9, a national antiwar gathering, the Assembly of Unrepresented People, as it was called, drew some 2,000 participants. There a much smaller meeting of antiwar activists from around the country decided to set up a National Coordinating Committee to End the War in Vietnam. The NCC scheduled a convention during the Thanksgiving weekend in Washington, D.C. This is the conference referred to in the FBI's "Open Letter."

The socialist assessment of the antiwar movement is contained in *Revolutionary Strategy in the Fight Against the Vietnam War,* a collection of articles and documents recently published by the SWP National Education Department.

It contains a transcript of a June 25, 1965, SWP Political Committee discussion that envisioned the main lines along which the movement would develop.

Jack Barnes, who is today the SWP national secretary, described the main divisions that would emerge within the movement. "They'll be over the question of exclusion versus non-exclusion and the question of unconditional opposition to the war. They'll take place over the question of subordinating the demands of the antiwar movement to the demands of 'progressive' politicians."

Drawing their initial inspiration from preparations for the April 17 march and then spurred on by the continuing escalation of both the war and antiwar activity, there was a proliferation of "Committees to End the War in Vietnam," or "CEWVs." They looked to the upcoming Thanksgiving conference as the first real opportunity to meet on a national level, compare notes, and chart future activity.

The gathering was marked by a major dispute, one that was confusing to most of the people there. The form of the fight was over a seemingly simple organizational matter, but in the background loomed two entirely different perspectives for the future of the new movement. In reality, a fundamental question was involved—whether the antiwar movement would remain and grow as an independent force in American political life or whether it would be channeled into Democratic party politics, a graveyard for social protest movements.

From the new independent antiwar committees had come a number of people, including many SWP and YSA members, who were interested in discussing the possibility of forming a national organization composed of committees standing for immediate withdrawal of American troops from Vietnam. The NCC did not purport to be such an organization—its purpose being to coordinate activities of all sorts of organizations opposed to the war, most of which at that time favored calling for a negotiated settlement.

The SWP and YSA did not propose eliminating the role of the NCC. They recognized a place for an organization that drew all opponents of the war together for common action, but they also saw a place in the coalition for a formation of independent committees favoring immediate withdrawal.

A proposal to add a workshop to the conference agenda for participants interested in setting up such an organization was met by an almost hysterical response from the conference steering committee. To the thousands who have over the years attended subsequent national antiwar conferences, where the right to hold the workshop of one's choice was accepted as a matter of course, this may seem hard to believe.

But the steering committee, in which the Communist party had a major influence, steadfastly refused to allow a "thirteenth" workshop. Those upholding what they saw to be their democratic right to meet on a question of mutual interest were forced to hold a "caucus" to discuss the subject.

Charges of "Trotskyite splitters and wreckers" were hurled left and right in order to obscure any rational discourse on the matter in dispute. The "splitter and wrecker" chorus continued for some time in several periodicals and in radical circles around the country.

Among the most vocal was the Communist party. Their perspective for the new movement was to send it out to ring doorbells for various Democratic party "peace candidates." The Stalinists correctly saw a national organization of independent committees calling for immediate withdrawal as an obstacle to that goal. The CP's insistence on the negotiation slogan, which violated the right of the Vietnamese to settle their own affairs, was tied into their Democratic party orientation, since it was a demand that many liberal Democratic candidates found acceptable.

The political questions in dispute would be widely discussed in the coming months and years. Over time the antiwar movement would be won to support immediate withdrawal, the demand most in line with the needs of both the American and Vietnamese peoples.

Supporters of an organization of independent committees favoring withdrawal were among the founders of the Student Mobilization Committee to End the War in Vietnam in 1966.

Without the eventual clarity over the course of the antiwar movement that resulted from the political fight that erupted at the Washington conference, it is safe to say that this country would not have seen the mass movement that, combined with the heroic struggle of the Vietnamese, forced the United States out.

The FBI, of course, was unable to get the SWP and YSA to pull out of the movement. Ignoring the "advice" of the FBI, the socialists discussed and drew their own conclusions on the meaning of the conference.

Among the most enlightening was the contribution made by SWP founder James P. Cannon before the Los Angeles branch of the SWP in December 1965. His remarks are also published in the publication mentioned above.

The NCC conference marked the first head-on confrontation between the new generation of SWP members and the Communist party. Cannon thought this was significant. Referring to the "Bring the Troops Home Now" slogan, he said, "I think our comrades were correct to adopt that slogan and their militancy at the conference and their refusal to be bluffed or bulldozed is quite admirable. All the more so that they were perhaps taken by surprise and hadn't had previous experience with what the perfidy of Stalinism and the Social Democracy is really like. I will guarantee you that they will never be taken by surprise again.

"These are permanent assets which speak well for the future," Cannon observed.

He made an observation that seems even more true ten years later. "Out of [the antiwar movement] I think we can see the beginnings of a new radical movement which raises great perspectives of world-historical significance for America."

*   *   *

It was not inevitable that a mass movement against the war in Vietnam would develop in this country. In fact, the life of the organized antiwar movement was characterized by frequent reevaluations of perspectives. On more than one occasion questions of strategy were posed that had life-and-death implications for the movement.

Their opponents within the antiwar movement would sometimes accuse members of the Socialist Workers party and the Young Socialist Alliance of possessing limited imagination. This charge stemmed from the socialists' continuing insistence on mass demonstrations as the way to end the war.

In the end, however, it turned out not to be the socialists who were short on imagination, but those who lacked confidence in the possibility of the American people taking to the streets in large numbers to demand an end to the war.

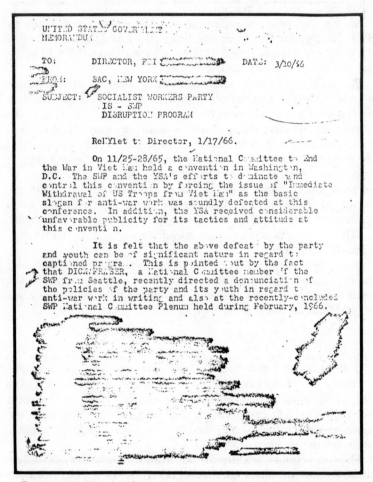

UNITED STATES GOVERNMENT
MEMORANDUM

TO: DIRECTOR, FBI   DATE: 3/10/66

FROM: SAC, NEW YORK

SUBJECT: SOCIALIST WORKERS PARTY
           IS - SWP
           DISRUPTION PROGRAM

ReNYlet to Director, 1/17/66.

On 11/25-28/65, the National Committee to End the War in Viet Nam held a convention in Washington, D.C. The SWP and the YSA's efforts to dominate and control this convention by forcing the issue of "Immediate Withdrawal of US Troops from Viet Nam" as the basic slogan for anti-war work was soundly defeated at this conference. In addition, the YSA received considerable unfavorable publicity for its tactics and attitude at this convention.

It is felt that the above defeat by the party and youth can be of significant nature in regard to captioned program. This is pointed out by the fact that DICK FRASER, a National Committee member of the SWP from Seattle, recently directed a denunciation of the policies of the party and its youth in regard to anti-war work in writing and also at the recently-concluded SWP National Committee Plenum held during February, 1966.

Pages 116-121: As the movement against the Vietnam War developed, the Socialist Workers party and the Young Socialist Alliance came to play a leading role in its left wing, eventually winning the majority of the movement over to their concept of holding massive, peaceful demon-

116

In all probability, the recent split of the Seattle Branch from the party together with the possible future splits of other branches and/or individual members is based in part on disagreements with the party leadership on anti-war policy.

Viewed in the light of the party's unsuccessful endeavors in various fields during the past decade, this recent venture appears to culminate a series of leadership policies which have caused dissention and rifts within the party.

To explait this, an anonymous letter has been prepared which could be directed nationally to selected party members who have some misgivings in regard to the leadership and direction of the party; however, to date, have not definitely made a break.

This letter would subsequently be directed to representatives of outside groups, particularly anti-war organizations after the original distribution. This distribution would contain an attached anonymous note, which would read:

"Understand this had wide circulation among Trotskyites. Have you seen it?"

It is felt the original distribution to selected party members be mailed from the Boston, Mass., Chicago, Ill., and San Francisco, California, areas where no particular party factions exist, however, areas which embrace a considerable number of party members. This would preclude immediate blame on any particular party member or group and lend credence to the possession of addresses of party members in these geographical areas. The subsequent mailing to anti-war committees and opposing radical groups would then be mailed 4 days hence from NYC. It is felt that many individuals from the NYC area would have access to addresses of these organizations on a national basis.

Within 10 days, the receiving offices are requested to furnish the names and addresses of approximately 20 per cent of the membership of the respective SWP membership, including those who have expressed some degree of past dissatisfaction with party policy.

strations for immediate withdrawal of U.S. forces. This operation's central aim was to demoralize members over a supposed series of failures in order to "seriously hamper" their efforts to build the antiwar movement.

Receiving offices are also requested to furnish the NYO the names and addresses of local or national anti-war committees that exist within their respective territories.

One copy of a sample of the anonymous letter is attached for receiving offices. If Bureau authority is granted to implement this suggestion, the anonymous letter will be mimeographed and prepared on commercial paper. The letter and addressed envelopes will then be afforded the Boston, Chicago and Los Angeles Offices for mailings from locations which would not bring suspicion to the Bureau.

It is believed that the above action will definitely create disruption within the ranks of the SWP, particularly on local levels and eventually cause considerable unrest in National Headquarters. Moreover, this action should seriously hamper the party's total occupation at this time, that is, its anti-war actions and objectives.

-3-

"AN OPEN LETTER TO TROTSKYITES"

You're a Trotskyite.

You've struggled through the years attempting to
influence others with your particular line of revolutionary
socialism. You've seen your Party's membership cut time and
time again by a seemingly endless series of splits, to the
point where, historically, the SWP has become known as the
"party of splits".

During the late 1950's, you entered, with your
party, into a regroupment effort with dissident ex-CPers who
were disillusioned over the crushing of the Hungarian
Revolution and the Khrushchev Revelations of the 20th
Congress of the CPSU. You watched as your party shunned the
true principles of regroupment on a common ground and
unsuccessfully attempted to dominate and recruit, thus gaining
the reputation as "spoilers".

You then picked up your chipped marbles and plunged
into the support of the Cuban Revolution by taking dead aim
on the Fair Play For Cuba Committee. Your party succeeded
in placing its "professional secretary", Berta Green, into
the FPCC leadership. You didn't have to wait long, however,
before your party's "raiding" operation within the FPCC on
a national basis became evident. So, it wasn't too much of
a surprise when Berta was bounced from the FPCC and your
party once again was accused of a crude attempt to "take
over" rather than provide constructive assistance to a most
worthy cause.

Far from dismayed, you next created the "independent"
Committee To Aid The Monroe Defendants, with the expectations
of reaching the Negro with the party line. Naturally, you
placed Berta Green, now available, as secretary of this
committee. Your party then proceeded, under the cloak of
pseudo-respectability, to implement its ultimate aims of
domination and recruitment. This activity necessitated
considerable effort on your part, but eventually incurred
nothing but the wrath of honest independents. To make it
worse, you had to absorb the responsibility for the loss of
funds and the creation of actual public harm to these victims
in Monroe, North Carolina ----- to the end that you were made
to suffer public attack and disavowal by no less than the
defendants themselves. A most disheartening episode on
behalf of the oppressed victims of the racist state, but
still, the SWP was the only existing Trotskyist party,
wasn't it? So you hung on.

*The FBI's elaborate efforts to discredit the SWP's role in the
Monroe committee, referred to in this "open letter," are
documented in chapters 4 and 7. Berta Green (now Berta
Langston) is an SWP member who helped initiate defense
efforts for the Cuban revolution and the Monroe defendants.*

In recent years, your party has taken a page from
the book of Stalin by its purges of party members who have
attempted to present for discussion alternative viewpoints
of current situations. Thus, your party was responsible,
in effect, for the creation of additional splinter groups
including the "Spartacist" movement which has attained
considerable renown in the radical community.

Presently, you've been struggling with your party
in its efforts to become part of the greatest ground swell
of opposition to this country's imperialist policies that
has ever existed. To this end, you had high hopes as the
party's youth arm, the Young Socialist Alliance, was
dispatched to Washington, D. C. last Thanksgiving to
participate in anti-war conferences and a massive
demonstration of protest to U. S. intervention in Vietnam.
Surely, this was an unprecedented opportunity to militate
against Washington and Wall Street. But, true to the SWP's
history of sectarianism, you witnessed the young "Trots"
promote a divisionary and undermining line of "immediate
withdrawal" at these conferences.

Prophetically, you saw your party and its youth
soundly defeated at this conference in yet another attempt
to recruit through division and domination.   Your attempt
to "save face", following this debacle, was the promotion
of a Caucus of "independent" anti-war committees based solely
on immediate withdrawal of U. S. forces in Vietnam. And
you justly suspect now that this tactic is viewed by radicals
and independents alike as a "paper front" composed of
committees hastily formed and led by YSA members throughout
the country. The people publishing and contributing to
"The Newsletter" of this Caucus only too well confirm this
fact.

Your ultimate dismay was recently realized when
your party and its movement was bitterly attacked by Fidel
Castro as "splitters and agents of imperialism". Thus, you
have been made to suffer the final irony. Your party, which
has posed as one of the leading defenders of the Cuban
Revolution, now finds itself in the most ironic position of
defending itself from a scathing attack by Castro himself!

Such is the state of affairs and mind in which you
now find yourself ----- sick with the realization that your
party and its youth have finally achieved utter disrespect
by all those whom it has strived to influence.

Your humiliation in the public and radical press is
now complete as you sadly observe your FORMER party press on.

Memorandum

TO : DIRECTOR, FBI ⬛⬛⬛⬛⬛⬛ DATE: 8/30/66

FROM : SAC, NEW YORK ⬛⬛⬛⬛⬛⬛

SUBJECT: SWP
IS-SWP
DISRUPTION PROGRAM

ReNYlet to Director 7/6/66.

The reported reactions of the SWP and actions taken as reported to date, regarding the anonymous mailings referred to in relet have been afforded the Bureau.

During recent months the SWP, particularly in the NYC area, has noticeably decreased its emphasis on activity within local anti-war committees. Party emphasis in this regard at this time amounts to the placing of one comrade in each committee in the event something of interest to the Party occurs in regard to any one of these committees. This slackening of emphasis in the placing of many comrades in these committees has not been explained to the general Party membership to date.

In a recent confidential memorandum prepared by the Political Committee of the SWP, the Party referred to a condition of dichotomy as existing within the various anti-war committees and organizations and considered itself as the left organization participating in these committees. It is felt, therefore, that the Party has experienced considerable difficulty in achieving its aims and objectives within these committees which may in part have resulted from information furnished these committees through the anonymous mailings.

It is further noted that a Party leader recently stated that the SWP must, under all circumstances, not "antagonize" any elements in the anti-war movement inasmuch as the Party "has always been accused of splitting", which accusation greatly upsets the Party. In this regard the above confidential memorandum also sets forth that the Party should make certain concessions with other radical organizations in order that they will not be accused of diversionary tactics. This is considered by the Party as its "new political tactic" In view of the above, it is felt that the Party's influence and prestige within the anti-war movement is of a tenuous nature at this time.

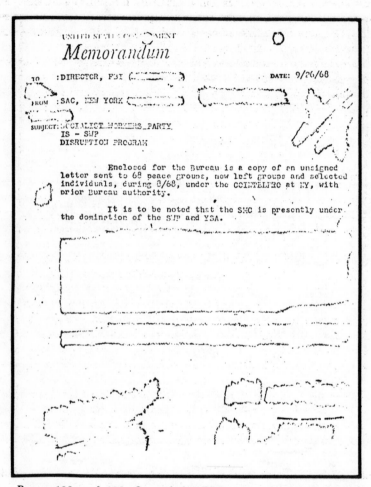

UNITED STATES GOVERNMENT

Memorandum

TO : DIRECTOR, FBI ( )   DATE: 9/26/68

FROM : SAC, NEW YORK ( )

SUBJECT: SOCIALIST WORKERS PARTY
IS - SWP
DISRUPTION PROGRAM

        Enclosed for the Bureau is a copy of an unsigned letter sent to 68 peace groups, new left groups and selected individuals, during 8/68, under the COINTELPRO at NY, with prior Bureau authority.

        It is to be noted that the SMC is presently under the domination of the SWP and YSA.

Pages 122 and 123: One of the FBI's many efforts to split and derail the antiwar movement was this 1968 red-baiting attack on the Young Socialist Alliance. The anonymous

122

WHO BUSTED SMC'S ASS?

Events since the disaster on June 29-30, have again demonstrated that everything the YSA touches turns to pure horseshit. Kipp Dawson and her gang of hypocrites took poor old SMC apart, changed all the pieces around, and put it back in the form of a sterile YSA group. Useless talk and parliamentary procedure is the new name of the game.

We who had served SMC from the beginning shed a few bitter tears, packed our bags and left. Linda Morse had the vision too. She saw through the Trotskyite shit and followed her nose through the door. She wasn't alone either. Many others, including Resistance, WRL, SDS and the Du Bois Clubs, followed her into the clear. So, we formed the Radical Organizing Committee to deal with issues related to the dirty war in Vietnam, the draft, racism and campus complicity. We wonder how long it will be before YSA takes a bead on the ROC?

We admit to a few hangups - mostly financial - but the Trotskyites have had many for years. There's the street-meeting hangup. We suspect that any SMC activity in the future will be in the form of YSA street meetings - zero contributions to the ending of the Johnson war. While the Trotskyites talk and talk, the war goes on and on.

All of which builds to a fine point - known to most of the independents in SMC for a long time. The old-line organizations have completely dried up....nothing but dust between the ears. Let's face it, the contributions of the SWP, YSA and FL to the movement have been minimal to say the least. The CP died of old age several decades ago, although we understand Gus is living real well.

We think ROC has something new to offer - a new approach to the problems of our times, a new light on the rise of radical consciousness within the student movement. This time, baby, the fascist tactics of the YSA are not going to get the chance to wreck the organization. No more committee packing and other high handed crap so neatly done by the Trotskyites. YSA can stick with its own hangups. We don't want 'em!

With it all, you have to admire the way YSA operated. Kipp and Syd were beautiful....just beautiful. They stuffed their platform up our collective asses smiling all the while. They were pained when we left. Kipp still looks pained.

We'll work for ROC now. Let's see what happens. A final word for YSA. "You busted our ass. You and you alone. Good luck mothers."

- Peace

letter singles out the YSA's advocacy of street demonstrations, encouraging the idea that these made "zero contributions to the ending of the Johnson war."

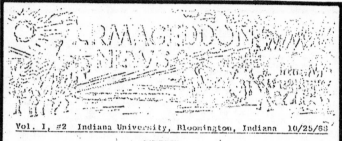

Vol. I, #2 Indiana University, Bloomington, Indiana 10/25/68

PURPOSE

As set out in our first "Armageddon News" issue, we students are concerned for the need for truth within our antiwar movement at Indiana University. As students, we feel the war in Vietnam is a political and military travesty, foisted on the American people by an unsympathetic administration, an administration unmindful of the will of the people. This situation, we can, and should deal with at the polls. The truth of the situation here at IU, however, is that this dissatisfaction with national policy is being used by a few to seize the university and to strike at the heart of the democratic system. We will simply point out the truth of this situation and you be the judge.

The Committee to End the War in Vietnam (CEWV)

Last year, members of the CEWV made an attempt to take over an academic building at IU, assaulting the police and violating the law in the process. They apparently thought that they were "different" and "above the law." This group felt free to use illegal methods to achieve their end. The big question now is just what was that end? Of the 35 arrested, all were convicted.

Last semester, Russell Block and Mark Ritchey set up a puppet by the name of Eric Shepard to act as Chairman of the CEWV. If you will look closely, you will find that Block and Ritchey, both members of the Young Socialist Alliance, pulled the strings for Shepard to jump. These people are the "manipulators" at IU and have the greatest influence on the "New Left" through the CEWV.

Last semester, Block and Ritchey announced the CEWV sponsorship of a series of lectures on "Socialism" and "The Communist Manifesto." These lectures were given, in part,

Pages 124 and 125: The second issue of Armageddon News, published and distributed secretly by the FBI for two semesters at Indiana University in Bloomington. It purport-

by an officer of the Young Socialist Alliance, Ralph Levitt, a former IU student. Levitt is now the State Chairman of the Socialist Workers Party's campaign and is presently running for Senator on the Socialist Workers Party ticket in the State of Indiana. What we want to know is what relationship do the topics "Socialism" and "The Communist Manifesto" have to do with a free people's rights and attempts to protest the policy of their government.

If this is the way the CEWV is to act, let's not be duped by its name. It's no longer a committee to end the war in Vietnam, no longer a forum for just dissent. It's a recruiting ground for subversion.

We all want an end to this war and we have a right to protest our government's participation therein. Ask yourself, then, what can be the true purpose of those who want to use your name and your energy for their objectives. It's surely worth your time and your effort to inquire penetratingly into organizations and causes that entreat your support.

A case in point is that the campus newspaper on 9/24/68 reported that CEWV is making plans to support the "International Days of Solidarity," planned by the Student Mobilization Committee (SMC) for the week of 10/21/68, and a large antiwar demonstration planned at IU for 10/26/68. Let's find out who we are declaring ourselves in solidarity with and what this Student Mobilization Committee really is. It wouldn't be surprising to find a considerable covey of SWP'ers behind it.

"DON'T LET THE NEW LEFT WIN THE ARMAGEDDON AT IU"

ed to be the work of antiwar students "concerned for the need for truth," but its right-wing slanders had no effect on genuine students opposed to the war.

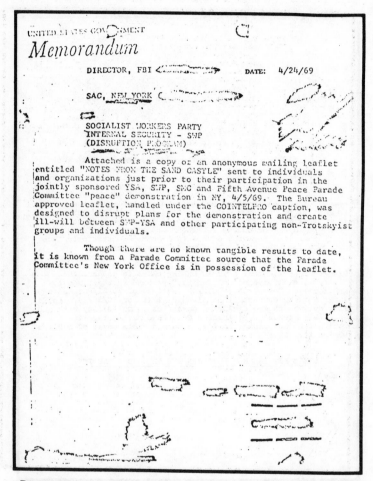

UNITED STATES GOVERNMENT

Memorandum

DIRECTOR, FBI   DATE: 4/24/69

SAC, NEW YORK

SOCIALIST WORKERS PARTY
INTERNAL SECURITY - SWP
(DISRUPTION PROGRAM)

     Attached is a copy of an anonymous mailing leaflet
entitled "NOTES FROM THE SAND CASTLE" sent to individuals
and organizations just prior to their participation in the
jointly sponsored YSA, SWP, SMC and Fifth Avenue Peace Parade
Committee "peace" demonstration in NY, 4/5/69. The Bureau
approved leaflet, handled under the COINTELPRO caption, was
designed to disrupt plans for the demonstration and create
ill-will between SWP-YSA and other participating non-Trotskyist
groups and individuals.

     Though there are no known tangible results to date,
it is known from a Parade Committee source that the Parade
Committee's New York Office is in possession of the leaflet.

*Pages 126 and 127: This 1969 FBI operation was designed to
"disrupt plans for the demonstration and create ill-will" by
red-baiting and ridiculing mass marches. The last para-*

126

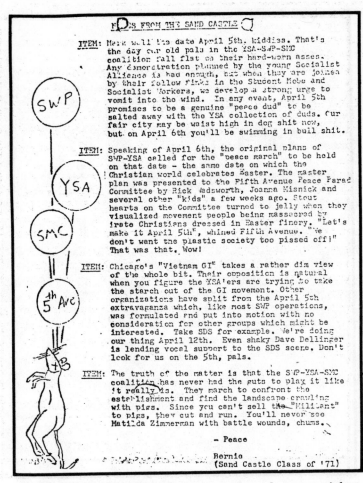

N🌞S FROM THE SAND CASTLE ◯

ITEM: Mark will the date April 5th, kiddies. That's the day our old pals in the YSA-SWP-SMC coalition fall flat on their hard-worn asses. Any demonstration planned by the young Socialist Alliance is bad enough, but when they are joined by their fellow finks in the Student Mobe and Socialist Workers, we develop a strong urge to vomit into the wind. In any event, April 5th promises to be a genuine "peace dud" to be salted away with the YSA collection of duds. Our fair city may be waist high in dog shit now, but on April 6th you'll be swimming in bull shit.

ITEM: Speaking of April 6th, the original plans of SWP-YSA called for the "peace march" to be held on that date - the same date on which the Christian world celebrates Easter. The master plan was presented to the Fifth Avenue Peace Parade Committee by Rick Wadsworth, Joanna Misnick and several other "kids" a few weeks ago. Stout hearts on the Committee turned to jelly when they visualized movement people being massacred by irate Christians dressed in Easter finery. "Let's make it April 5th", whined Fifth Avenue. "We don't want the plastic society too pissed off!" That was that. Wow!

ITEM: Chicago's "Vietnam GI" takes a rather dim view of the whole bit. Their opposition is natural when you figure the YSA'ers are trying to take the starch out of the GI movement. Other organizations have split from the April 5th extravaganza which, like most SWP operations, was formulated and put into motion with no consideration for other groups which might be interested. Take SDS for example. We're doing our thing April 12th. Even shaky Dave Dellinger is lending vocal support to the SDS scene. Don't look for us on the 5th, pals.

ITEM: The truth of the matter is that the SWP-YSA-SMC coalition has never had the guts to play it like it really is. They march to confront the establishment and find the landscape crawling with pigs. Since you can't sell the "Militant" to pigs, they cut and run. You'll never see Matilda Zimmerman with battle wounds, chums.

                                    - Peace

                                    Bernie
                                    (Sand Castle Class of '71)

graph of the "newsletter" in particular advocates violent confrontations with police.

OPTIONAL FORM NO. 10
MAY 1962 EDITION
GSA FPMR (41 CFR) 101-11.6

UNITED STATES GOVERNMENT

Memorandum

TO : DIRECTOR, FBI ⟨⟩ DATE: 1/21/70

FROM : SAC, ATLANTA

SUBJECT: COINTELPRO - NEW LEFT
IS

     During the past several months, Socialist Workers Party/Young Socialist Alliance and Atlanta Revolutionary Youth Movement/Students for a Democratic Society have been so uncooperative as the two largest factions in a "coalition" of Atlanta New Left and pacifist groups banded together to make a bigger and better local showing in anti-war demonstrations, that most of the demonstrations have been unsuccessful and disappointing to participants. "The Great Speckled Bird", Atlanta's New Left newspaper, has run several articles during the past six months which referred to "coalition" meetings as "pitiful meetings," pointing out that the "stupid bickering" between the two factions made the group" a"paper coalition " of "extremely limited usefulness." This situation was instrumental in keeping the morale in Atlanta's anti-war movement at a low ebb, as evidenced by the fact that an estimated 125 persons from the entire area participated in the anti-war demonstration in Washington, D. C., on 11/15/69, after much effort by the "coalition", which had originally chartered nine buses to carry participants and was talking about having as many as 1000 people in Washington.

     However, since ARYM/SDS allegedly dropped their affiliation with SDS in late November, 1969, and became merely "RYM", they have allegedly apologized to the "coalition" for their uncooperative attitude in the past and have indicated a willingness to cooperate with the "coalition" in local anti-war activities. This was apparently evidenced in an Atlanta anti-war conference held on 1/17/70, at which RYM was well represented, and DAVID SIMPSON of the RYM leaders, was appointed as Co-coordinator of a forthcoming anti-war type demonstration to be held in Atlanta during

Pages 128 and 129: Alarmed by plans for a united demonstration, the FBI wrote an anonymous letter to a Revolutionary Youth Movement leader claiming he was

the anticipated visit of Vice President SPIRO AGNEW on
2/21/70, after SIMPSON had been defeated by a YSA member
in an election for the position, his appointment as
Co-coordinator being then suggested by a local SWP/YSA
leader.

It would appear that it would be greatly
to the Bureau's advantage not to let these two major
factions in the Atlanta anti-war movement become overly
friendly and cooperative. It is, therefore, suggested
that the Bureau authorize the mailing of the following
anonymous letter to DAVID SIMPSON:

"Dear Dave,

"How can you RYM people be so naive and
gullible as to continue to let the Trots run
the whole show their way as they did again at
the anti-war conference at Emory. It looks
like you could see that they have the whole
thing figured out, and have all the answers
before these so-called "conferences" even
start.

"As a communist, which they say you are,
you sure don't show any knowledge of communist
tactics. Why don't you check out your Trot
friends on the night before your "conference,"
and you might find that they are together,
busy with plans as to how they will manipulate
the coalition to their own specifications --
being gracious enough to throw you a few
scraps to keep you happy.

"Our revolution is a long way off if
we have to wait for them to do it their way--
they've been carrying the ball for years, now
it should be someone else's turn. .

"A Friend "

2

being manipulated by the YSA. The purpose was "not to let
these two major factions in the Atlanta antiwar movement
become overly friendly and cooperative."

Memorandum

TO : DIRECTOR, FBI 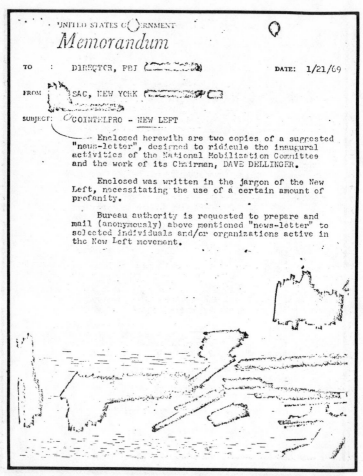 **DATE:** 1/21/69

FROM : SAC, NEW YORK

SUBJECT: COINTELPRO - NEW LEFT

    -- Enclosed herewith are two copies of a suggested "news-letter", designed to ridicule the inaugural activities of the National Mobilization Committee and the work of its Chairman, DAVE DELLINGER.

    Enclosed was written in the jargon of the New Left, necessitating the use of a certain amount of profanity.

    Bureau authority is requested to prepare and mail (anonymously) above mentioned "news-letter" to selected individuals and/or organizations active in the New Left movement.

Pages 130 and 131: This anonymous mailing, in addition to personal ridicule of antiwar leader Dave Dellinger, attempt-

DESPERATE DAVE DANGLES DINGUS

Murderously Mangles MOBE

Washington, D. C. Jan. 20 - Speaking in his usual high pitched voice, Dave Dellinger, National Chairman of the National Mobilization Committee (MOBE), today claimed that the anti-inaugural demonstrations called by his organization had been responsible in getting the Paris peace talks going again.

Dellinger made this startling disclosure before an audience of newsmen in the dingy Hawthorne School which housed many of his followers. A cluster of the latter stood behind their Guru sniffling and fingering wilted flowers. Dellinger, looking pale - more fairy-like than ever - tried to control the squeaks in his voice to no avail. "How many demonstrators did MOBE bring to the inaugural?", he was asked.

"At least 10,000, " he answered.

"Bullshit", was heard in several sections of the room.

Dellinger shuffled his notes. " Let's make that 5,000."

"Bullshit".

"Would you believe 3,000?" Silence. Dave rolled his eyes at the ceiling. "I'm not going to play at numbers, " he chirped. "What matters is that MOBE accomplished so much. We did get the peace talks going. We did break some windows in the National Geographic Society building. Despite police brutality, our brave people managed to throw cans and sticks at the President." His voice went higher - sounding like glass bells in a soft summer breeze. "We shook the establishment, gentlemen."

Associated Press stood up. "We understand MOBE is broke. That you lost control of the thing. That SDS and many other organizations in the peace movement refused to back you. That you have no idea how MOBE funds were spent."

Dellinger put a finger in his mouth and sucked it reflectively. Some minutes passed before he spoke. "MOBE is solvent, boys. As of this morning, we have $1.54 in the treasury. The price of peace is high." He tried to look grim. "SDS, of course, is just a bunch of dirty college kids with grass for brains. We didn't want them or need them." He formed his lips into a cute bow. "I must go now. We're hitching a ride back to New York today unless we can raise bus fare."

He shoved four fingers into his mouth and was led slowly from the room humming "We Shall Overcome."

ed to spread suspicion over the use of movement funds and create friction between MOBE and SDS.

It is now clear that the rulers of this country watched all this very closely. We have direct evidence that on at least several occasions the FBI sought to intervene in the political life of the movement in order to widen splits and to further trends that were harmful to the movement's development.

From 1968 to 1970 the Indianapolis office of the FBI waged a two-year campaign to destroy the antiwar movement, the YSA, and other radical groups at Indiana University in Bloomington. For this crusade the FBI created a newsletter called *Armageddon News*.

Published surreptitiously over two semesters, the newsletter's purpose, according to the FBI, was to "prevent any nonLeftist students from being duped into joining the groups of the New Left."

In a memo not reproduced in this book, the national headquarters told Indianapolis that "the next issue (Volume 1, Number 2) and subsequent material must contain a more sophisticated approach with regards to the situation at Indiana University and in relation to the broad protest movement in this country. Your leaflet should be prepared ostensibly by students who, while disagreeing with the Vietnam war policy and so forth nevertheless deplore subversive elements on and off campus who are using these issues for their own purposes."

Despite such efforts by Washington to edit it into an apparently liberal-leaning publication with some appeal to the students it was aimed at, *Armageddon News* came off as a right-wing scandal sheet, as the reproduction included in this chapter shows. According to former students at Indiana University, it had zero impact on the antiwar movement there.

In addition to publishing and distributing the newsletter, the FBI infiltrated the YSA in Bloomington in order to bring about a "split in philosophy" in what it characterized as the only group on campus with a "degree of organizational structure."

In another case, in Atlanta, the FBI intervened in order to reopen a split that was in the process of being healed. The FBI feared that, after a period of disagreement in the local antiwar coalition, the Revolutionary Youth Movement (RYM, a split-off from the Students for a Democratic Society) was going to cooperate with the YSA in organizing antiwar activities. To try to prevent this, the Atlanta FBI sent an anonymous letter to a RYM leader charging manipulation of RYM by the "Trots."

During August 1968, the FBI mailed out an anonymous leaflet purporting to be from a supporter of the Radical Organizing Committee. The ROC was a short-lived organization formed by Communist party members and others who, after unsuccessfully attempting to exclude members of the YSA from the national staff of the Student Mobilization Committee to End the War in Vietnam, themselves left the SMC.

The leaflet praises those who split from the SMC and red-baits the YSA for "committee packing and other high handed crap so neatly done by the Trotskyites."

At the center of this controversy were Kipp Dawson and Syd Stapleton, two YSA members on the SMC staff who had become prominent antiwar leaders. Dawson now works as a printer, and Stapleton is national secretary of the Political Rights Defense Fund, which is sponsoring the suit that pried loose the evidence of FBI intrigue. The *Militant* discussed with them the 1968 dispute in light of the news about the FBI's role.

The SMC had been established in the fall of 1966 by a variety of forces, among them members of the Young Socialist Alliance, radical pacifists, and members of the Communist party and of its youth group at the time—the DuBois Clubs. The CP had from the beginning been a reluctant partner in the coalition, in part because its participation violated its traditional sectarian taboo against working with "Trotskyites."

By 1968 the SMC had already established itself as a major organization, with chapters on many campuses. It had brought out thousands of young people on the day of the largest demonstration held up to that time—April 15, 1967.

"Where the CP was headed didn't come out in a clear way until the 1967 year-end SMC convention in Chicago," Stapleton remembered. "They put forward a number of proposals that would have shifted the emphasis of the SMC away from the war. The effect would have been to turn it into a liberal youth group that dealt with many issues. During the approaching election campaign, such a group could easily swing into supporting liberal Democrats."

Things didn't come to a head until after the successful SMC-sponsored student strike against the war in April 1968. The election pressure was building, and the Eugene McCarthy presidential campaign was beginning to attract some antiwar activists. At the same time, the United States opened peace talks with the Vietnamese in Paris as part of a move to defuse antiwar sentiment. Some opponents of the war thought negotiations would bring a rapid end to the fighting.

"A controversy broke out in the 'working committee,' which was a semiofficial body of SMC members living in New York," Dawson recalled. "It was decided that no member of any political 'tendency' or group would be allowed on the SMC staff. That meant Syd and I were fired."

The antiwar movement had been based on "nonexclusion," the idea that all opponents of the war were welcome regardless of their political affiliation. The Stalinists of the Communist party defended this new step, which reversed that policy, in a variety of ways, often contradictory or illogical. For example, Mike Zagarell said YSAers should be excluded because their work had succeeded in "narrowing" the coalition.

What was really happening, of course, was that the CP was trying to transform the SMC into a support group for liberal Democratic "peace candidates," as they were called. They needed to get rid of the YSA to make that possible.

"The working committee resolution was adopted with the backing of pacifists, the Communist party, and their supporters," Stapleton said. "They had a mechanical majority."

This action brought a wave of protests from SMC members around the country. The CP and the rest of the exclusionists had opened the fight on a narrow organizational level, with the political differences submerged. They continued this by refusing to schedule an SMC convention in the Midwest, which had been mandated by the previous SMC convention. Finally, an SMC Continuations Committee meeting was set in New York—the main base of the exclusionists.

"They had tried in every way imaginable to avoid an open political discussion of the issues," Dawson said. "Now 400 people were gathered at the continuations committee meeting. The discussion was at last beginning. Suddenly, a thirty-three-year-old public relations man named Art Goldberg, who had somehow gotten himself on the SMC working committee, jumped up on a table and shouted, 'This is a Trotskyite-dominated conference! All the independents are leaving!'"

A minority began walking out chanting "Up against the wall!" They were met by a counter-chant of "Bring the troops home now!"

"The whole fight was summed up by the chants that came from

the two sides," Stapleton remarked. "The FBI's leaflet was definitely in their style."

The SMC went on to become bigger than ever. In the fall of 1969, and then in the spring of 1971, it was the co-organizer of the biggest antiwar demonstrations in American history. Its February 1970 conference drew almost 4,000.

What happened to those who walked out? Sixty of them met at a New York church to discuss what to do. As one of them aptly put it, "Although we all feel like brothers because we all hate the Trots, that isn't enough of a basis for a new organization." Phyllis Kalb of the CP summed up the mood there. "I'm against the YSA concept of mass demonstrations. I'm just tired of them." They finally decided to form the Radical Organizing Committee.

"The last I heard of ROC was during the demonstrations at the Democratic party convention in Chicago that summer," Stapleton said. "I spotted two people passing out a ROC leaflet."

Stapleton recalled a later incident. "I was in Washington earlier this year at a picket line demanding an end to continued funding for the fighting in Vietnam. A person I didn't know walked up to me and said, 'I just wanted to let you know that you were right.' 'Right about what?' I asked. 'You were right about the war in 1968,' he replied. 'You see, those of us who set up ROC really thought the war was over. I thought it had ended and it was time to go on to other issues. But it turned out you were correct.'

"He was a high school student in 1968 who had gotten drawn into the fight," Stapleton continued. "He is now a reader of the *Militant*."

Immediately prior to the April 5, 1969, antiwar demonstrations, the FBI mailed out another leaflet to an unknown number of individuals and groups that were opposed to the war. "Notes from the Sand Castle," as it was titled, red-baited the YSA and SWP and criticized them for failing to take on the "pigs."

Would such a leaflet have had any credibility? Unfortunately, it probably would because in it the FBI advocated a viewpoint that enjoyed some support at the time, primarily in circles around Students for a Democratic Society. The anonymous author claimed to be an SDS member.

In the leaflet the FBI argued in favor of violent confrontations. The following June SDS would break up, and the strongest advocates of these tactics would become the Weathermen.

When the SDS National Council opened its March 28-30

meeting in Austin, Texas, that year, the 200 delegates and several hundred more observers were handed an open letter from the YSA. "The central task of revolutionary youth right now," the YSA wrote, "is to build the April 5-6 demonstrations [against the war] as large and as militant as possible."

This was precisely what YSA members around the country were doing. But the SDS gathering had what they considered to be more important business before them.

The Austin meeting marked a turning point for SDS. For several years, the Progressive Labor party, then the country's largest Maoist group, had been an increasingly important factor in the political life of SDS. With the deepening radicalization on campus, the grouping around the SDS national office was having more and more trouble responding to the political questions raised by the PLP.

At Austin they were ready to unveil the weapon they hoped would meet the PLP's challenge. They unexpectedly emerged as full-fledged followers of Chairman Mao himself, and of Stalin too. It was really just about that simple. Why let the PLP have a monopoly on Mao Tse-tung thought?

It was here that Robert Avakian, now leader of the Revolutionary Union, made his national debut as an exponent of Maoism. The same is true of SDS national office member Mike Klonsky, today an officer of the October League.

The Maoists have tried to portray themselves as the most ardent defenders of the Vietnamese revolution. It is worth noting that in Austin not only did they fail to endorse the April action, SDS did nothing at all about the war.

Nevertheless, the demonstrations turned out to be quite significant and sizable. New York saw 100,000 march in the rain. There were 50,000 in San Francisco, 30,000 in Chicago, 4,000 in Atlanta, and more in other cities.

They served notice on the ruling class that the American people were not taken in by the negotiations in Paris. Nixon's talk of an impending "settlement" was not going to get him off the hook.

It is no exaggeration to say that it was the stubborn persistence of the SWP and YSA and others who agreed with them in arguing for the tactic of mass peaceful protests that kept the movement alive. Ultimately, the FBI and those that it serves were unable to hold the movement back from its goal.

7 Red-baiting

In the last chapter we saw some examples of the FBI's use of red-baiting in the antiwar movement—smearing its targets as "subversives," "manipulators," or whatever else would appeal to the prejudices of the intended audience.

The different varieties of this technique are such a mainstay of FBI sabotage that it is worth studying them in somewhat more detail.

The documents on the following pages are concerned with five different Cointelpro operations. Four involve the use of red-baiting to disrupt the antiwar movement and the Black civil rights movement. The fifth operation was designed to intensify hostility between the Socialist Workers party and the Communist party.

• The first set of documents includes an obscene, sexist leaflet, purportedly issued by an opponent of the war in Vietnam. This leaflet was mailed to a large number of antiwar activists. It calls for excluding the Young Socialist Alliance and the Socialist Workers party from the national antiwar coalition.

Its purpose, in the FBI's words, was "to cause disruption in the peace movement, primarily in the New Mobilization Committee to End the War in Vietnam, and to minimize the growing influence of the SWP in the movement."

• The next selection from the FBI files involves an attempt to cause the NAACP to withdraw its endorsement of the Committee to Aid the Monroe Defendants (CAMD) in 1962. (Another operation against the CAMD is described in chapter 4.)

The national NAACP had not endorsed the CAMD, but some local chapters had. The FBI mailed an anonymous letter to

NAACP Executive Secretary Roy Wilkins falsely charging that the CAMD "was set up, dominated, and controlled by the Socialist Workers Party." The letter insinuated, without offering a shred of evidence, that CAMD funds were being misused by the SWP.

• The third set of documents concerns the campaign of Sam Jordan, a Black candidate for mayor of San Francisco in 1963. He ran independently of the Democratic party, and the SWP extended support to his campaign. The FBI mailed an unsigned letter that, in their words, was "ostensibly from a longshoreman who wants to vote for Jordan because of Jordan's strong stand for Negro rights but the writer is concerned because of all the known Socialist Workers Party (SWP) members who are running Jordan's campaign."

• Fourth is an anonymous "memorandum" from "a member" of the National Steering Committee of the New Mobilization Committee, an antiwar coalition. The "memo" charges that the "Trotskyites . . . have seen fit to use the good offices of the NMC to further their own political aspirations, nebulous as they are."

• Finally, there is a 1962 directive from FBI headquarters in Washington to its New York office instructing them to try to stir up friction between the SWP and the Communist party. The *Worker,* the newspaper reflecting the views of the Communist party at that time, had recently run an advertisement containing the address of the New York SWP offices as a location to purchase tickets for a benefit for the Irish movement. The FBI telephoned the *Militant* and the *Worker* in order to provoke animosity around this ad. It is interesting to note, in the FBI's evaluation of this operation, that the *Militant* editor did not rise to the bait.

These documents do not, it should be remembered, tell the whole story. The FBI is refusing to turn over many of its files. We can assume that some of them contain information about more recent Cointelpro operations, such as those directed against the women's movement.

Also, the FBI is refusing to release any documents or sections of documents that it claims reveal "investigative techniques." "Investigative techniques," we know, include bugging, wiretapping, mail tampering, and burglaries. The present documents have been censored to remove these unsavory aspects of FBI work. It is also well known that the FBI uses its undercover agents in various movements to encourage violence, disunity, and red-baiting attacks, but that is only hinted at here.

These papers do prove that the FBI has found red-baiting to be one of its most effective weapons against struggles which the rulers of this country are out to destroy.

The FBI uses red-baiting in two ways. The first is more familiar, and we have already seen some examples. Information is fed to newspaper columnists and politicians who are sympathetic to the FBI. For example, during the movement against the war in Vietnam, on the eve of a demonstration, some columnist or newspaper would suddenly "reveal" that socialists were active in organizing the demonstration.

The purpose would be to create the impression that socialists were secretly controlling the action for their own ulterior motives. This was intended to scare people away from coming out to oppose the war. The Cointelpro papers contain examples of the FBI's use of the news media in this way.

The documents reproduced in this chapter show the other way the FBI employs red-baiting. The message and the objective are the same. The difference is that the red-baiting seems to be coming from supporters of the Black, antiwar, or labor movements.

The FBI tries to initiate or encourage the exclusion of socialists, who are depicted as dishonest individuals who lack a sincere concern for the movement and are not to be trusted.

The FBI's aim is to turn people away from fighting their enemy and toward fighting each other.

Why did the FBI think it could get results with these methods? The reason is that anticommunist prejudices run very deep in this society.

These prejudices have their roots in the anticommunist hysteria which began in the late 1940s and continued, although weakened, into the 1960s. The anticommunist witch-hunt coincided with the cold war between the United States and the Soviet Union. Americans were taught that communism was evil incarnate and that godless communists were out to rule the world. This was necessary to convince the American people to support massive war expenditures, go along with wars like those in Korea and Vietnam, and maintain a huge standing army to act as world policeman for capitalism.

At home, this campaign meant that socialists and communists had to be driven out of public life. Venal politicians—like Nixon—built political careers on the anticommunist issue.

Memorandum

TO : DIRECTOR, FBI ⬚⬚⬚⬚⬚ DATE: 2/13/70

FROM : SAC, NEW YORK ⬚⬚⬚⬚⬚

SUBJECT: SOCIALIST WORKERS PARTY - DISRUPTION PROGRAM IS-SWP

ReNYlet, 12/30/69.

Enclosed for the Bureau is a copy of an unsigned leaflet entitled "Fly United?", mailed this past week to some 230 selected individuals and organizations in New Left and related groups under the COINTELPRO at New York with prior Bureau authority.

The leaflet is designed to cause disruption in the peace movement, primarily in the New Mobilization Committee to End the War in Vietnam, and to minimize the growing influence of the SWP in the movement. It is also designed to cause consternation and confusion in the SWP itself.

The enclosed has been marked "Obscene" because of its contents. The copy program on the leaflet has been written in the jargon of the New Left, necessitating the use of a certain amount of profanity.

Copies of the leaflet have been mailed to members of the SWP, its youth group the Young Socialist Alliance, the Student Mobilization Committee, CP USA, DCA and other groups.

No tangible results have been detected at this early date, although one source, ⬚⬚⬚⬚⬚ has attributed the leaflet to dissident elements in the New Mobilization Committee.

The Bureau will be kept advised of reported results.

Pages 140 and 141: In 1970 the FBI mailed a red-baiting leaflet, ostensibly from an antiwar activist, to "cause

disruption in the peace movement . . . and to minimize the growing influence of the SWP."

OFFICIAL FORM NO. 10

UNITED STATES GO~

Memorandum

TO : Mr. ~~~~~~~~~~~~~~~~~ DATE: 5-14-62

FROM : Mr. ~~~~~~~~~~~~~~~~~

SUBJECT: SOCIALIST WORKERS PARTY
INTERNAL SECURITY - SWP
DISRUPTION PROGRAM

New York by airtel dated 5-10-62 recommended that an anonymous telephone call be made to an official of the National Association for the Advancement of Colored People (NAACP) which has recently endorsed the Committee to Aid the Monroe Defendants (CAMD) to advise this official that the CAMD is run on a day-to-day basis by the Socialist Workers Party (SWP), which has been designated pursuant to Executive Order 10450. and thereby cause considerable disruption of the CAMD's activities. If the NAACP became aware of the control of the CAMD by the SWP, any financial help and other support would be withdrawn by the NAACP.

~~~~~~~~~~~~~~~~~ the CAMD recently received endorsement and financial support from the NAACP. ~~~~~~~~~~~~~~~~~ The SWP now feels that the CAMD has become a "legitimate" organization through support of the NAACP.

The leadership of the NAACP is undoubtedly unaware of the fact that the SWP created and directs the CAMD. The SWP is attempting to raise money as soon as possible to organize a move of headquarters of the CAMD from the SWP building, 116 University Place, New York City, to separate quarters to avoid CAMD's connection with the SWP becoming known. It is felt that if the NAACP were aware of this connection support would be withdrawn.

New York proposes to place an anonymous telephone call to ~~~~~~~~~~~~~~~~~ the NAACP ~~~~~~~~~~~~~~~~~
~~~~~~~~~~~~~~~~~ New York purposes placing this call ~~~~~~~~~~~~~~~~~
~~~~~~~~~~~~~~~~~ advised that the CAMD was being operated from SWP headquarters and directed on a day-to-day basis by Berta Green, SWP member, and CAMD secretary. ~~~~~~~~~~~~~~~~~ pass this information on to appropriate leaders of the NAACP in view of the NAACP's support recently extended to the CAMD. ~~~~~~~~~~~~~~~~~

Pages 142-148: A 1962 operation aimed at destroying the Committee to Aid the Monroe Defendants by claiming it was secretly controlled by the SWP for ulterior purposes. Washington approved New York's plan for an anonymous

Memorandum to [REDACTED]
RE: SOCIALIST WORKERS PARTY

[REDACTED] this information would be verified by a visit to SWP headquarters, 116 University Place, New York City.

[REDACTED] The SWP intends to use this committee to make a national and international issue out of charges lodged against Robert Franklin Williams and other individuals who were involved in a racial incident during demonstration: held at Monroe, North Carolina, on 8-27-61. Williams was charged with interstate flight to avoid prosecution on charges of kidnapping a white couple at gunpoint and is reportedly in Cuba. The SWP has been organizing branches of the CAMD throughout the United States where branches of the SWP exist.

It is felt that this operation should be approved since the possible withdrawal of NAACP support would have considerable disruptive effect upon the SWP and cause considerable damage to future SWP activities in the civil rights field.

[REDACTED] advised that a letter has been directed to an official of the NAACP containing this information. Such a letter should be signed as being from a true friend and supporter of Negro rights.

RECOMMENDATION:

That the attached airtel to the New York Office be approved authorizing the disruption program operation as outlined above and instructing New York [REDACTED] that a letter had been sent to an NAACP official containing similar information. Precautionary statements are included.

phone call to the NAACP, cynically suggesting that it be coupled with a letter from "a true friend and supporter of Negro rights."

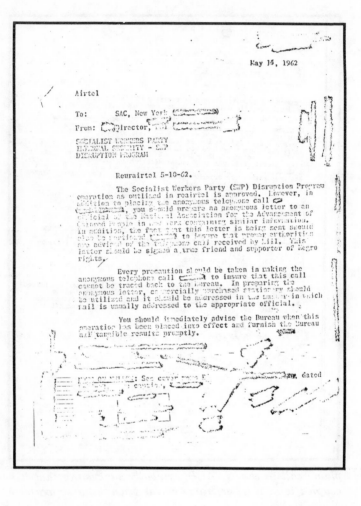

May 14, 1962

Airtel

To: SAC, New York (

From: Director, FBI

SOCIALIST WORKERS PARTY
INTERNAL SECURITY - SWP
DISRUPTION PROGRAM

Reurairtel 5-10-62.

The Socialist Workers Party (SWP) Disruption Program operation as outlined in reairtel is approved. However, in addition to placing the anonymous telephone call you should prepare an anonymous letter to an official of the National Association for the Advancement of Colored People in New York containing similar information. In addition, the fact that this letter is being sent should also be mentioned to insure that proper authorities are advised of the telephone call received by mail. This letter should be signed a true friend and supporter of Negro rights.

Every precaution should be taken in making the anonymous telephone call to insure that this call cannot be traced back to the Bureau. In preparing the anonymous letter, commercially purchased stationery should be utilized and it should be addressed in the manner in which mail is usually addressed to the appropriate official.

You should immediately advise the Bureau when this operation has been placed into effect and furnish the Bureau any tangible results promptly.

NOTE ON YELLOW: See cover memo

144

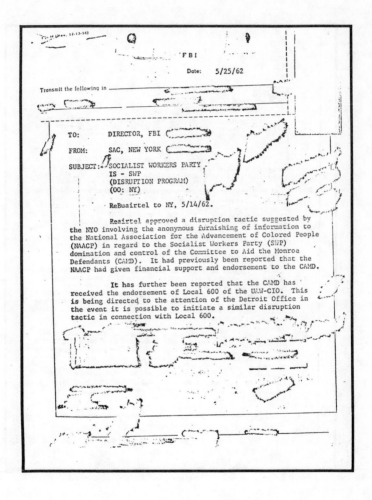

FBI

Date: 5/25/62

Transmit the following in _____

TO: DIRECTOR, FBI

FROM: SAC, NEW YORK

SUBJECT: SOCIALIST WORKERS PARTY
          IS - SWP
          (DISRUPTION PROGRAM)
          (OO: NY)

ReBuairtel to NY, 5/14/62.

Reairtel approved a disruption tactic suggested by the NYO involving the anonymous furnishing of information to the National Association for the Advancement of Colored People (NAACP) in regard to the Socialist Workers Party (SWP) domination and control of the Committee to Aid the Monroe Defendants (CAMD). It had previously been reported that the NAACP had given financial support and endorsement to the CAMD.

It has further been reported that the CAMD has received the endorsement of Local 600 of the UAW-CIO. This is being directed to the attention of the Detroit Office in the event it is possible to initiate a similar disruption tactic in connection with Local 600.

AIRTEL TO BUREAU

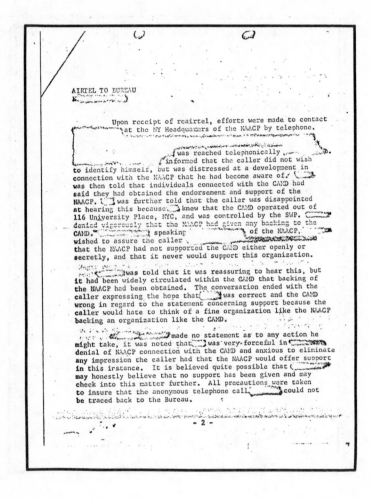

Upon receipt of reairtel, efforts were made to contact ~~~~~~~ at the NY Headquarters of the NAACP by telephone. ~~~~~~

~~~~~~~~~~~~ was reached telephonically ~~~~~~~~~~. ~~~~~~~~~~~ informed that the caller did not wish to identify himself, but was distressed at a development in connection with the NAACP that he had become aware of. ~~~~~ was then told that individuals connected with the CAMD had said they had obtained the endorsement and support of the NAACP. ~~~ was further told that the caller was disappointed at hearing this because ~~~ knew that the CAMD operated out of 116 University Place, NYC, and was controlled by the SWP. ~~~~~ denied vigorously that the NAACP had given any backing to the CAMD. ~~~~~~~~~~~ speaking ~~~~~~~ of the NAACP, ~~~~ wished to assure the caller ~~~~~~~~~~~~~~~~~~~~~~~~~ that the NAACP had not supported the CAMD either openly or secretly, and that it never would support this organization.

~~~~~~~~~~~~ was told that it was reassuring to hear this, but it had been widely circulated within the CAMD that backing of the NAACP had been obtained. The conversation ended with the caller expressing the hope that ~~~~ was correct and the CAMD wrong in regard to the statement concerning support because the caller would hate to think of a fine organization like the NAACP backing an organization like the CAMD.

~~~~~~~~~~~~~~~~~~~~~ made no statement as to any action he might take, it was noted that ~~~ was very forceful in ~~~~~~~ denial of NAACP connection with the CAMD and anxious to eliminate any impression the caller had that the NAACP would offer support in this instance. It is believed quite possible that ~~~~~~~~ may honestly believe that no support has been given and may check into this matter further. All precautions were taken to insure that the anonymous telephone call ~~~~~ could not be traced back to the Bureau.

- 2 -

As suggested by the Bureau in reairtel, the phone
call was followed up by an anonymous letter which was prepared
on commercial stationery and mailed at a distance from the
FBI Office to Mr. ROY WILKINS, Executive Secretary, NAACP,
20 West 40th Street, NYC. This letter set forth the following:

"Dear Sir:

"An outfit I have some knowledge of, the Committee
to Aid the Monroe Defendants, has been boasting lately how
they've been made 'legitimate' through the endorsement and
financial support of the NAACP.

"No one can deny that the Negro people in Monroe
need assistance, but it's a shame that it is tied in with the
CAMD.

"You may not have much dealings with the so-called
Negro nationalist groups uptown, but many of their leaders
could tell you how CAMD was formed.

"It was set up, dominated, and controlled by the
Socialist Workers Party, the Trotskyist branch of the communist
movement. They use Conrad Lynn as a front man, but CAMD is run
by Berta Green, of the SWP. Green was thrown out as secretary
of the Fair Play for Cuba Committee to get rid of SWP influence
but she bounced right into CAMD. Now the NAACP is supporting
what even the FPCC didn't want to be smeared with.

"Ask anyone who has worked with CAMD where the paper
work is done, where the mailings are prepared, where a lot of
the Monroe contributions are stored. It's the second floor
of 116 University Place, which if you don't know, is the SWP
hall. Maybe with money from NAACP they've been able to move to

- 3 -

"a different office by now, but if not, go see for yourself.

"It won't do the work of the NAACP in the South a bit of good if it's known its funds and good name are backing a group in the pocket of the SWP.

"A true friend and supporter of Negro rights"

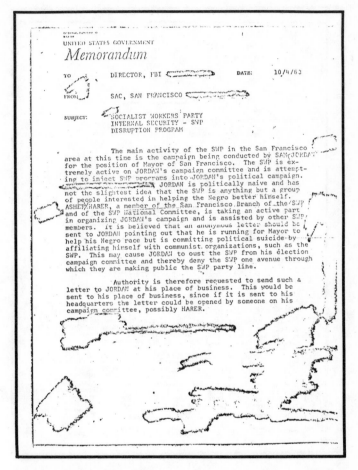

OPTIONAL FORM NO. 10
5010-104

UNITED STATES GOVERNMENT

Memorandum

TO : DIRECTOR, FBI   DATE: 10/4/63

FROM : SAC, SAN FRANCISCO

SUBJECT: SOCIALIST WORKERS PARTY
INTERNAL SECURITY – SWP
DISRUPTION PROGRAM

     The main activity of the SWP in the San Francisco
area at this time is the campaign being conducted by SAM JORDAN
for the position of Mayor of San Francisco. The SWP is extremely active on JORDAN's campaign committee and is attempting to inject SWP programs into JORDAN's political campaign.
JORDAN is politically naive and has
not the slightest idea that the SWP is anything but a group
of people interested in helping the Negro better himself.
ASHER HARER, a member of the San Francisco Branch of the SWP
and of the SWP National Committee, is taking an active part
in organizing JORDAN's campaign and is assisted by other SWP
members. It is believed that an anonymous letter should be
sent to JORDAN pointing out that he is running for Mayor to
help his Negro race but is committing political suicide by
affiliating himself with communist organizations, such as the
SWP. This may cause JORDAN to oust the SWP from his election
campaign committee and thereby deny the SWP one avenue through
which they are making public the SWP party line.

     Authority is therefore requested to send such a
letter to JORDAN at his place of business. This would be
sent to his place of business, since if it is sent to his
headquarters the letter could be opened by someone on his
campaign committee, possibly HARER.

*Pages 149-152: The FBI's 1963 attempt to have socialists
kicked out of an independent Black candidate's campaign
committee with a red-baiting letter ostensibly from a longshoreman.*

UNITED STATES GOVERNMENT

Memorandum

TO : DIRECTOR, FBI   DATE: 10/10/63

FROM : SAC, SAN FRANCISCO

SUBJECT: SOCIALIST WORKERS PARTY
IS - SWP
DISRUPTION PROGRAM

Re Bulet dated 10/8/63.

Set forth below is a proposed anonymous letter to be
sent to SAM JORDAN in an effort to force him to oust the SWP
from his election campaign committee.

It is to be noted that ASHER HARER, JAMES NICKLAS,
HAYDEN PERRY, and CONNIE HANN, who are mentioned in the letter,
are members of the San Francisco Branch of the SWP, while AARON
CHAPMAN and ALLEN WILLIS are not SWP members. However, WILLIS
is a former SWP member and CHAPMAN has long been very close to the
SWP and is amenable to SWP control. If JORDAN will oust all of
these people from his campaign, the SWP will be shut out from this
campaign and it will nullify all of the SWP's recent efforts in
San Francisco.

Set forth below is the proposed letter: (Errors in spelling
in the letter are intentional)

October ___, 1963
San Francisco, Calif.

Dear Mr. Jordan,

First of all, let me apologise for sending this letter
without any name on it, but I am a longshoreman and would not like
to have Asher Harer know I am writing this. If he knew he could
make things pretty tough for me on the waterfront.

When you indicated that you were running for Mayor of
San Francisco to represent negros and other groups who have never
been properly represented in San Francisco government I was
delighted. However, after attending some of your meetings and
noticing who is runing your campaign I have come to the conclusion
that you are committing political suicide by allowing people like
Harer (a long time wheel in the Socialist Workers Party - the
Trotsky communist party) and his stooges Nick Nicklas, Hayden Perry,

Connie Hann, Aaron Chapman, and Allen Willis to run your campaign. By leting them run your campaign you are indicating to the public that you support communism and that if I support you, then I too support communism. Now I have no intention of being branded as a "red" and I know a lot of other people, negro and white, who will not continue to support you in this election unless you publicly denounce the SWP and completely cut them out of your campaign.

You have a big following in San Francisco and could really do a job in the local political picture. Please don't ruin everything by allowing yourself to become a tool of the SWP.

Sincerely,

Disappointed

P.S. Harer is really using you as a pipe line for the commie line.

SAC, San Francisco ⌇⌇⌇⌇⌇⌇   10/21/63

Director, FBI ⌇⌇⌇⌇⌇⌇

SOCIALIST WORKERS PARTY
INTERNAL SECURITY - SWP
DISRUPTION PROGRAM

Reurlet 10/10/63.

Authority is granted for you to prepare and then
anonymously mail the letter set out in relet to San Jordan
who is running for the office of Mayor of San Francisco as an
independent Negro candidate.

The letter should be handwritten on a cheap grade
of tablet paper and contain the spelling errors set out in
the sample letter enclosed with relet. It should be mailed
to him in care of his place of business.

Take the usual precautions to prevent the preparation
of the letter and the subsequent mailing of it from being
associated with the Bureau. Advise the Bureau when the letter
has been mailed and then be alert for any tangible results.

NOTE:

The anonymous letter is ostensibly from a longshoreman
who wants to vote for Jordan because of Jordan's strong stand
for Negro rights but the writer is concerned because of all the
known Social Workers Party (SWP) members who are running Jordan's
campaign. The letter indicates unless Jordan gets rid of the SWP
members. many people who don't want to be branded as a "Red" will
not support Jordan. The writer of the letter indicates therein he
knows Asher Harer, a main spokesman for Jordan, and if the writer
identified himself, Harer could make things tough for the writer
on the waterfront. The letter has definite disruptive potential.

Reference is made to New York letter dated 1/14/70.

Enclosed are two copies of a suggested "memorandum" concerning the National Steering Committee of the New Mobilization Committee To End The War In Vietnam (NMC), which is designed to cause splits within NMC leadership by pitting the non-Trotskyites against radicals who are members of the Socialist Workers Party (SWP). It is also designed to bring to the fore the small number of Blacks actually serving on the steering committee.

Bureau authority is requested for New York to prepare enclosed memorandum and mail anonymously to all members of the NMC Steering Committee and other selected officals in the organization. Copies will also be sent to selected officals of the Vietnam Moratorium Committee in Washington, D. C.

Pages 153 and 154: "To cause splits within NMC," the FBI in 1970 sent a fake letter blaming the SWP for alleged exclusion of Blacks from the antiwar coalition.

NEW MOBILIZATION COMMITTEE TO END THE WAR IN VIETNAM
1029 Vermont Avenue, N. W., Washington, D. C. 20005
Area Code 212 737-8600

MEMO TO: National Steering Committee

RE: The Absolute Racial Imbalance of The NSC

Having for a short time served as a member of the NSC, and currently active in the Moratorium Committee - both in Washington and New York, I find it necessary to call attention to certain facts overlooked or shovelled under the rug by NMC leadership.

My understanding at the time I joined NMC was that it was to be run as a non-exclusionary organization - devoted to one primary cause, the immediate end of the frightful war in Vietnam. We were not to be side-tracked into supporting the aims of the militant left. We were not to be sucked into protests against the government's trial of the Conspiracy 8 in Chicago and the like. Our sights were to be adjusted at some later time when the war terminated. Or, so I thought.

Over the past several years the Trotskyites have literally taken control of the body proper and have repeatedly resisted efforts to recruit black brothers into NMC leadership. In addition, they have seen fit to use the good offices of the NMC to further their own political aspirations, nebulous as they are.

I have been sickened - on more than one occasion - by the promises made to the Black United Front, promises not kept, promises made with the mouth and not the heart. The attitude of the Steering Committee towards the BUF was and is a matter of disgrace. In the main, NMC leadership has been no better than the racist-politicians and phony-liberals who give lip service to the black community and turn their backs on any positive action.

The NMC leadership has demonstrated an appalling lack of sensitivity towards the largest minority in the country. If NMC is to survive the coming months, the situation must be rectified immediately. Our leadership - including the omni-present Trotskyites and other radicals - had better take positive steps before those who disagree with current policy, and there are many, either withhold future support or take their leanings elsewhere. NMC leadership, it is my belief, was NMC would greatly benefit under a leader like Sam Brown of MC.

To avoid senseless imbroglio, I choose to remain anonymous until the proper time. Just for the record - I am not Black.....

April 4, 1962

Airtel

To: SAC, New York (____)
From: Director, FBI ____

COMMUNIST PARTY, USA
COUNTERINTELLIGENCE PROGRAM
INTERNAL SECURITY - C

In the 4/1/62 issue of "The Worker" on page 10, an advertisement appears for a social affair to be held 4/5/62 at the Bitter End Cafe, 147 Bleecker Street, to commemorate one "Paddy Mohir, IRA hero - Union leader." The advertisement states tickets are available at three locations, one of which is listed as "Socialist Workers Party City Office - 116 University Place."

It has always been a firm policy of the Communist Party (CP) not to consider any cooperation with or assistance to the Socialist Workers Party (SWP) especially in the use of advertising space in the columns of "The Worker." This advertisement in the 4/1/62 issue must have been arranged through some contacts by "The Worker" staff with SWP members. This appears to offer an opportunity to carry out a counterintelligence operation.

New York should consider making an anonymous telephone call to "The Worker" office accusing the officials of becoming so capitalistic that they are getting financial support by giving advertising space to the SWP. It can also be pointed out that this situation will lead to the paper being infiltrated by the Trotskyites. New York can also consider an anonymous telephone call to SWP officials to make the accusation that some traitor must be doing business with the CP.

If it appears that a controversial issue is being created over this matter, security informants participating

Pages 155-157: A 1962 anonymous phone call operation to promote hostility between the Socialist Workers party and the Communist party, which were cooperating in defense of the Irish struggle.

Airtel to New York
RE: COMMUNIST PARTY, USA
    COUNTERINTELLIGENCE PROGRAM

in the Counterintelligence Program of your office should
be directed to raise further criticism of the CP's
abandonment of the long-standing principle of no
association with the SWP.

Advise the Bureau of the action taken by
your office. Promptly furnish any tangible results.

NOTE ON YELLOW:

Airtel is being used to enable the New York Office
to handle this matter while "The Worker" issue of 4/1/62
is still current.

- 2 -

UNITED STATES GOVERNMENT

Memorandum

TO : DIRECTOR, FBI (   )   DATE: 4/9/62

FROM : SAC, NEW YORK

SUBJECT: CPUSA
COUNTERINTELLIGENCE PROGRAM
IS-C

      ReBuairtel, 4/4/62, regarding an advertisement appearing in the 4/1/62 issue of "The Worker" which stated that tickets for a particular affair were available at the offices of the Socialist Workers Party (SWP) at 116 University Place.

      On 4/6/62, the NYO made a pretext call to "The Worker" and a person believed to be JAMES JACKSON was asked about this advertisement. JACKSON immediately indicated that he was aware of this and said it was due to an oversight and would not occur again. JACKSON was in complete agreement that it should not have appeared and promised that it would not occur again.

      The NYO immediately made a pretext call to "The Militant" and spoke to an individual who identified himself as an editor. The caller told him that he called "The Worker" to find out whether there was now cooperation with the SWP and then repeated JACKSON's answer. The caller then went on with a tirade about how "The Worker" demands and gets any advertising it wants in other newspapers and that "The Worker" is denying freedom to others by taking such an attitude. The editor was in complete agreement and said that it was a very interesting point. He was told to call "The Worker" and ask about the ad and he would receive the same answer. He was told that his paper should point out this incident to its readers to expose "The Worker's" denying freedom. The editor agreed but said that because of "The Worker's" troubles with the government at this time, if "The Militant" attacked them on such an issue, someone might think they were "putting the knife into them." The editor said he would discuss it with others on the staff. The editor displayed an interested and cooperative attitude.

Members of the Socialist Workers party, the Communist party, and other radical groups were thrown out of government jobs and out of the union movement. Pressure was put on Black organizations to exclude socialists from their ranks.

Hollywood churned out productions depicting Marxists as soulless agents of an alien force out to destroy America. If socialists or communists appeared to be working for some good cause, this was merely a clever trick to disguise their true aims and to win unsuspecting converts. A whole generation was weaned on this.

But the rise of the Black civil rights movement beginning in the late fifties and the mass antiwar movement of the sixties changed a lot of things.

The rulers began to find that the "Communist menace" was no longer sufficient to rouse Americans to die in Southeast Asia. Opponents of the Vietnam War learned that it was impossible to build a movement against a war that was justified by anticommunism while making concessions to anticommunist ideology within the movement itself. The principle of nonexclusion was established in the antiwar movement. Anyone could participate— be they Democrat, Republican, Communist, or Socialist—as long as they agreed with the goal of ending the war.

Much to the dismay of the FBI, the old-style anticommunism of the 1950s lacked the power to destroy the antiwar movement. Columnists Rowland Evans and Robert Novak could write on the eve of the April 24, 1971, antiwar demonstration that Socialist Workers party leader Fred Halstead was one of the central organizers of the action and have virtually no impact on the million people who turned out in Washington, D.C., and San Francisco.

While this type of red-baiting was becoming less and less useful, the FBI focused increasing attention on red-baiting that was made to appear as if it came from within the movement.

One of the reasons the FBI found this tactic so useful is that, unfortunately, some forces inside the movement engage in red-baiting as a substitute for political discussion.

This sometimes takes the form of charges that the SWP and YSA are "opportunist." What people who make this accusation are insinuating is that socialists are not really interested in furthering, for example, the antiracist struggle but are merely "using" it for some unspecified selfish end.

Red-baiting is almost invariably used in order to avoid or

obscure a discussion of real political differences. A recent example occurred at the February 14–16, 1975, antiracist conference in Boston. Some 2,000 people from across the country gathered to found a new organization, the National Student Coalition Against Racism. After a weekend of democratic discussion and debate, NSCAR voted overwhelmingly to help build the NAACP-initiated May 17 national march on Boston to support busing and desegregation of Boston schools.

A group led by members of some Maoist sects tried to disrupt the conference by charging that the whole affair was "dominated," "manipulated," and "controlled behind the scenes" by the "opportunists" of the YSA and SWP.

The disrupters delayed the conference for a while and finally decided to walk out. As they were leaving they said, "We demand an end to busing, an end to federal troops, and an end to this whole fucked-up reactionary conference!"

Then it became clear for all to see that their red-baiting slanders were simply a cover for their political opposition to a movement in defense of busing, which was the entire purpose of the desegregation conference.

Differences of opinion will arise in any healthy, living movement, and discussion of those political differences can only help make the movement stronger. Red-baiting poisons the atmosphere and makes discussion impossible. It sows the seeds of suspicion and distrust.

The FBI is well aware of this. These documents provide some important lessons. They show who benefits from red-baiting—the FBI, the racists, and the reactionaries. And they show who loses—the labor movement, the civil rights movement, and other movements for social change.

8 Firing teachers:
'The children and the country deserve to be protected'

In 1968 the FBI took special pride in railroading Walter Elliot out of his hobby. As scoutmaster of Troop 339 in Orange, New Jersey, the FBI reasoned that he posed "a distinct threat to the goal of the scouting movement."

Why? Walter Elliot was married to a socialist.

In the view of the bureau, this necessitated a Cointelpro operation to counteract his "strong influence in shaping the minds of young boys." The agent in charge of the effort called Elliot's removal a "successful application of the disruption program for a worthy cause."

The FBI sanctimoniously claims a special duty to "protect young minds." Protect them, that is, from ideas unpopular with the FBI. Teachers prove an obvious target with their strategic "access" to "fertile young minds," as one memo put it.

The Cointelpro files reprinted here show how this crusade to fire teacher activists dovetails with the FBI's relentless drive to harass and victimize the Socialist Workers party out of existence.

The case of Evelyn Sell involves an interstate, interagency conspiracy against a preschool teacher described, even by the FBI, as "an intelligent, excellent teacher who was well qualified in her field."

"The decision not to issue a new contract or consider the subject further for employment after the termination of her current contract is based upon information received from [deleted] the Austin Police Department."

That is how the FBI summed up its efforts in a March 31, 1970, FBI memorandum captioned "Evelyn Rose Sell, SM-SWP" (Subversive Matter—Socialist Workers party). This security matter was in actuality an FBI vendetta against Sell, a Head

161

Start teacher in Austin, Texas. The top-secret information referred to is the fact that in 1968 Sell ran for public office in Michigan as an SWP candidate.

This data was sniffed out by the FBI in Detroit at the request of the San Antonio office and was confidentially passed on to the Austin police, who then tipped off the Austin Independent School District. School officials, with this information in hand, refused to renew Sell's contract at the end of the 1970 school year.

Today, M.K. Hage, Jr., president of the Austin School Board, who served in that post when Evelyn Sell was fired, says that "the social climate was such that we would fire anyone who was a socialist."

In an interview, Evelyn Sell gave her side of the story.

Before moving to Austin in the summer of 1969, Sell had taught in the Head Start program in Detroit for four years. She had helped organize a special unit of the Detroit Federation of Teachers encompassing the preschool program, and had been a delegate to the 1969 Michigan Federation of Teachers convention in the spring of that year.

Sell's political beliefs were no secret. She joined the SWP in 1948 and had been active in socialist politics since then. She was nominated by the party several times as a candidate for public office.

"All my cards were on the table," says Sell. "It was the FBI and the Austin school district officials who were underhanded and secretive."

It wasn't until after the school district refused to renew her contract in 1970 that she became aware of the FBI's keen interest in her. The only indication before that time that the FBI was keeping tabs on her was an incident shortly after she moved to Austin.

Her son Eric, then a student at Austin High School and an activist in the Student Mobilization Committee, was called into his principal's office. There he was informed that the FBI had paid the school a visit and had told the principal of his antiwar activities. The principal warned Eric that he was not to organize any antiwar activities at school, and then added that they were aware that his mother was a teacher.

"Eric came home and told me about his 'interrogation,' and I said, 'Well, the FBI must be in contact with my school,' and I expected to hear something about it. But they never brought it out into the open."

The fall of 1969 saw massive protests against the war, and Austin was no exception with its large university population. Eleven thousand marched to the state capitol for the October 15 Moratorium. And organizing meetings on the campus would draw from 100 to 150 people. Sell was a consistent participant and organizer of these events.

Did she connect her antiwar activity with the decision not to renew her contract in 1970?

"I suspected at the time that the FBI may have had something to do with it. The school used the excuse that the Head Start program, which had been administered by the school district, was no longer to be under its control. But I knew that was a phony excuse," Sell recalls.

"Texas had passed a law establishing a kindergarten system for the first time in its history, and they had very few qualified teachers. As a matter of fact, they were scrounging around trying to find teachers who had kindergarten endorsements. I was one of the few who had such an endorsement from the Texas Education Agency. And I asked to be retained by the school district to teach in the new kindergarten program."

When Sell's contract was not renewed, she immediately applied to the new agency set up to direct the Head Start program, the Human Opportunities Corporation. She was accepted as an educational services supervisor. By early 1971 she had been promoted to director of the Child Development Program.

The FBI files released on Sell end with the notation that Sell had been hired by the HOC and that the information about her socialist activities would be furnished to that agency.

What the files don't report is that the FBI streamed in and out of the HOC offices, repeatedly visiting at least three of Sell's supervisors in an attempt to convince them that, qualified or not, this socialist did not deserve a job. One reason they offered was her active participation in the women's movement. Sell had played a leading role in organizing a demonstration in support of the right to abortion.

"The HOC directors were outraged by the visits," Sell says. "One of them told me that he was seriously considering filing a lawsuit against the FBI because of the harassing visits."

The HOC resisted the FBI pressure because they considered Sell an asset to the program. In her personal files, Sell has a letter from the parents' council of Head Start praising her for her work. It says in part:

"We wish to commend Mrs. Evelyn Sell . . . for a job *well done!* The fairness and efficiency in her willingness to always make herself readily available if she could be of any help in any situation was quickly recognized." (The emphasis is in the original.)

Sell left the Head Start program in January 1972, not because the FBI visits frightened or intimidated her, but because she was again to run for public office as a socialist in the 1972 elections.

"But I don't doubt that the FBI visits continued until the day I left," Sell comments. "And they certainly continued past the April 1971 'termination' of the FBI Cointelpros."

The Starsky Case

Prominent in the ranks of teachers victimized by the FBI is Morris Starsky. In 1970 the FBI encouraged Starsky's dismissal from his job as a professor of philosophy at Arizona State University. The Phoenix office of the FBI sent an anonymous letter slandering him to a faculty committee reviewing his teaching contract.

In a memo dated May 31, 1968, the Phoenix FBI noted that local targets for Cointelpro were "pretty obvious. . . . It is apparent that New Left organizations and activities in the Phoenix metropolitan area have received their inspiration and leadership almost exclusively from the members of the faculty in the Department of Philosophy at Arizona State University (ASU), chiefly Assistant Professor MORRIS J. STARSKY."

To that description of himself, Starsky adds that he helped organize the first antiwar teach-in at ASU; he led a campus free speech fight; he helped lead a successful campaign to win campus recognition for SDS; he participated in campus activities to support striking Tucson sanitation workers and a union organizing drive by Chicano laundry workers; he served as a presidential elector for the Socialist Workers party in 1968; he helped to reestablish the ASU chapter of the American Federation of Teachers; and he was the faculty adviser of the Young Socialist Alliance and the Student Mobilization Committee.

All that provoked quite a furor among right-wing state legislators and university regents. The Faculty Committee on Academic Freedom and Tenure (whose members received the FBI's slanderous letters) held a hundred hours of public hearings on whether Starsky was entitled to teach at ASU. Three thousand students and over 250 professors signed petitions supporting Starsky's right to academic freedom.

The committee's members were not duped by the FBI's anonymous slanders, although they expressed surprise five years later when they learned that "A Concerned Alumnus" was really J. Edgar Hoover. The committee voted unanimously against dismissing Starsky. But the regents refused to renew his contract and he lost his job in June 1970. Starsky says that "it's sort of like being found innocent and executed anyway." Since ASU he has lost two teaching jobs in California for political reasons.

Starsky calls the FBI drive against him an attack on the rights of everyone. "What teacher is safe?" he asks. "What ideas would not subject a teacher to this kind of attack?—only U.S. government approved ideas."

Starsky has spent the past five years fighting for his rights in and out of court. He has won one damage suit already. And an Arizona court ruled that the ASU action violated his civil rights. Meanwhile, the FBI refuses to turn over to Starsky some of its files on him on the grounds of "national security."

"I've taught a couple of logic courses," he says, "but I had a hard time figuring out how my seeing my own files would harm national security. After I read the Cointelpro documents it became clear: 'national security' means the FBI's security from the nation finding out the vicious things it does in violation of people's civil liberties."

More Poison Pen Letters

FBI schemes to get two other teachers fired are documented here. Unlike the Sell and Starsky cases, these efforts did not have the results the FBI wanted.

In 1969 the Detroit office received approval from Washington to send a series of letters on Professor David Herreshoff to Michigan State Senator Robert Huber. Huber was chairman of a legislative committee investigating student dissent on state campuses.

The letters were signed "A Fed-up Taxpayer!" They document seventeen years of Herreshoff's political activity from 1951, when he was a student at the University of Minnesota, through 1968, while he was a member of the faculty at Wayne State University.

Compiled from "public source material" to ensure the FBI could not be identified as the letters' source, the information was intended to make a case for ridding Wayne State of Herreshoff's "peculiar" influence.

Herreshoff's "disruptive" activities apparently included a debate with a former FBI agent in 1951 on the topic "Does the FBI Menace Civil Liberties?"; his participation in the University of Minnesota's Socialist Club, which spearheaded a campaign in 1955 to remove campus restrictions on outside speakers; and his election to the Detroit executive board of the American Civil Liberties Union. Herreshoff says that he is "happy that everything charged against me in the FBI 'denunciation' is true."

Herreshoff recalls that during the debate with the FBI agent he accused the agency of "breaking the law every day in the week. That was back in 1951. I guess the FBI never forgets an insult."

Herreshoff says he doesn't believe the FBI will ever change and it ought to be abolished. "Wouldn't abolishing the FBI be a fitting observation of the bicentennial of the revolution?"

In still another poison pen episode, the FBI tried in April 1969 to get Maude White (now Wilkinson) "separated from her employment" as a preschool teacher in Washington, D.C. The local FBI sent an anonymous letter signed "A Concerned Citizen," purporting to be from Wilkinson's neighbor, to the superintendent of the D.C. school system. The letter said that "Miss White has held weekly meetings of a socialist youth group" in her apartment.

After expounding upon the classical FBI distortions of the YSA as a group supporting "violent activities against established authority," the letter continues, "I bring this information to your attention in order to protect the D.C. School System from the menace of a teacher who does not have the interests of the children or the country at heart."

But it was precisely the interests of the children and the American people that led Wilkinson to become a socialist: "Being a teacher, especially in the D.C. schools, I saw how rotten the schools were, how much money was spent on war and how little on education," she says.

Wilkinson's files also document the three-way collusion between the FBI, the intelligence unit of the Washington police, and the school administration. According to an FBI memo, one local cop was delegated responsibility for conducting intelligence investigations within the D.C. school system at the direction of the assistant superintendent of schools in charge of personnel. Information on Wilkinson compiled by the D.C. police was forwarded to the FBI.

The Response From Teachers

The revelation of such attacks on teachers has evoked an outraged response from educators and civil libertarians alike. Professor William Van Alstyne, president of the American Association of University Professors, demanded that the agents responsible for the "sleazy and surreptitious campaigns" against Morris Starsky be fired. Delegates to the 1975 national convention of the AAUP gave the former professor a warm welcome and voted to support his efforts to defend academic freedom. Local chapters of the AAUP and the American Federation of Teachers cosponsored many of Starsky's speaking engagements during a nationwide tour he conducted in the spring of 1975 to win support for the SWP suit.

Publications with large circulations among educators, including *Higher Education Daily, Chronicle of Higher Education,* the AAUP's *Academe,* and the AFT's *American Teacher,* printed articles criticizing the Cointelpro attacks.

At the 1975 national convention of the 1.7 million member National Education Association, Executive Secretary Terry Herndon condemned the FBI's operations as "reminiscent of the witch-hunts during the McCarthy era," noting that nowhere does the FBI charge that any one of its targets was not a good teacher.

Herndon asked a question that must be on many people's minds: "While only a few such cases have surfaced thus far, we cannot help wondering how many more teachers were dismissed or harassed because of counterproductive surreptitious activity by the FBI into the private lives of educators." The NEA leader added, "Such efforts to get teachers fired only make the job of teaching about democracy and government that much harder."

The head of Maude Wilkinson's chapter of the NEA summed it up well. In a telephone interview, John Radcliffe told of his immediate response to the Cointelpro operations.

"As soon as I found out about the situation," Radcliffe said, "I called the school district and told them that . . . we, acting as the union, would absolutely and categorically not tolerate anyone messing with Maude's job."

Radcliffe has no doubt that the FBI is continuing its efforts to get people with dissident views fired. But he thinks that the political climate has changed and that the FBI doesn't have such an easy time of it today. "As far as Maude's job goes in Fairfax County, it's secure," Radcliffe concluded. "She can belong to any political party she wants to."

UNITED STATES GOVERNMENT

Memorandum

TO : DIRECTOR, FBI   DATE: 10/8/69

FROM : SAC, SAN ANTONIO

SUBJECT: COINTELPRO

RE: EVELYN ROSE SELL

On 10/3/69, _____ Austin Independent School
District, 6100 Guadalupe, Austin, Texas, advised that
EVELYN ROSE SELL _____
is a teacher in the Head Start Program under the
auspices of the Austin Independent School District.
_____ the school district desires to
terminate her services but is unable to do so because
of a lack of information from the Detroit Public School
System concerning her background.

LEADS:

DETROIT DIVISION:

AT DETROIT, MICHIGAN: Through established
sources, furnish information that can be disseminated,
with Bureau approval, _____

*Initial FBI memo suggesting the Detroit office seek out
information on Evelyn Sell that could be furnished to the
Austin, Texas, school board.*

168

The Head Start Program will be operated by an independent group commencing with the 1970-1971 school year and will no longer be under the auspices of the Austin Independent School District.

The subject was described as an intelligent, excellent teacher who was well qualified in her field.

Bureau attention is directed to San Antonio letter to the Bureau captioned "COINTELPRO, IS - DISRUPTION OF NEW LEFT," ▓▓▓▓▓▓▓▓▓▓▓▓▓▓▓▓▓▓▓▓▓▓▓ dated 1/13/70. ▓▓▓▓▓▓▓▓▓▓▓▓▓▓▓▓▓ the decision not to issue a new contract or consider the subject further for employment after the termination of her current contract is based upon information received from ▓▓▓▓▓▓▓▓▓▓▓▓▓ the Austin Police Department. ▓▓▓▓▓▓▓▓▓▓▓▓ information furnished ▓▓▓▓▓▓▓▓▓▓would be furnished to the organization which will be handling the Head Start Program in the 1970-1971 school year.

-3-

The third page of a March 31, 1970, memo reporting the success of the bureau's campaign to drive Sell out of her teaching job.

UNITED STATES GOVERNMENT

Memorandum

TO : DIRECTOR, FBI DATE: 10/20/70

FROM : SAC, SAN ANTONIO

SUBJECT: EVELYN ROSE SELL
IS - SWP

On 10/5/70, _____, Austin
Independent School District, Austin, Texas _____, advised
that the subject is not employed by the Austin Independent
School District. He stated that it was his understanding
that she is employed by the Human Opportunities Corporation (HOC)
in the Head Start Program, (HSP).

On 10/19/70, ALEX PORTER, Office of General Counsel
for Office of Economic Opportunity (OEO), advised that the
subject is employed by the HOC as Director of the HSP, Austin,
Texas, and that she resides at 2700-B Matthews Drive, Austin,
Texas. Mr. PORTER stated that the HOC is a private, nonprofit
corporation which is funded by OEO.

*This memo, tracing Sell to her new Head Start job, lays the
groundwork for continued harassment.*

170

FROM :   SAC, PHOENIX ⟨‾‾‾‾‾⟩ (b)(7)

SUBJECT: COUNTERINTELLIGENCE PROGRAM
                  INTERNAL SECURITY
                  DISRUPTION OF THE NEW LEFT

          ReBulet to Albany, 5/10/68, copies to all offices.

          On the basis of developments to date, it is apparent
that New Left organizations and activities in the Phoenix
metropolitan area have received their inspiration and
leadership almost exclusively from the members of the faculty
in the Department of Philosophy at Arizona State University
(ASU), chiefly Assistant Professor MORRIS J. STARSKY. The
most logical targets for potential counterintelligence action
locally are therefore pretty obvious.

          STARSKY in presently the subject of active invest-
igation in the Selective Service category, ▓▓▓▓▓▓▓. (b)(7)
▓▓▓▓▓▓▓▓▓▓▓▓▓▓▓▓▓▓▓▓▓▓▓▓▓▓▓▓▓▓▓▓▓▓▓▓ (b)(6)
Background information which is thus developed may prove
useful for counterintelligence purposes. ▓▓▓▓▓▓▓
▓▓▓▓▓▓▓▓▓▓▓▓▓▓▓▓▓▓▓▓▓▓▓▓▓▓ (b)(7) (b)(6)
▓▓▓▓▓▓▓▓▓▓▓▓▓▓▓▓▓▓▓▓▓.

          STARSKY has already received considerable publicity
in Phoenix papers in connection with his anti-war and antidraft activities. ▓▓▓▓▓▓▓▓▓▓▓▓▓▓▓▓▓ (b)(6)
▓▓▓▓▓▓▓▓▓▓▓▓▓▓▓▓▓. This suggests an
avenue of counterintelligence approach as well as that offered
by reliable and cooperative contacts in the news media.

                  The remainder of this 3 page
                  communication does not concern
                  Morris Starsky.

          (b)(7)

Memorandum

TO : DIRECTOR, FBI ( ) (b)(7) DATE: 10/1/68

FROM : SAC, PHOENIX ( ) (b)(7)

SUBJECT: COUNTERINTELLIGENCE PROGRAM
INTERNAL SECURITY
DISRUPTION OF THE NEW LEFT

Remylet, 7/1/68.

1. Potential Counterintelligence Action

MORRIS J. STARSKY, by his actions, has continued
to spotlight himself as a target for counterintelligence
action. He and his wife were both named as presidential
electors by and for the Socialist Workers Party when the
SWP in August, 1968, gained a place on the ballot in Arizona. In addition they have signed themselves as treasurer
and secretary respectively of the Arizona SWP. Professor
STARSKY's status at Arizona State University may be affected
by the outcome of his pending trial on charges of disturb-
ing the peace. He is alleged to have used violent, abusive
and obscene language against the Assistant Managing Director
of Gammage Auditorium at ASU during memorial services for
MARTIN LUTHER KING last April. Trial is now scheduled for
10/8/68 in Justice Court, Tempe, Arizona.

A recommendation for counterintelligence action
as to STARSKY will be submitted by separate letter.

> The remainder of this 2 page
> communication does not concern
> Morris Starsky.

172

Bureau approval is requested to mail a copy of the enclosed anonymous letter to each member of the faculty committee which is hearing the charges against STARSKY. This committee is sitting in the Law School on the ASU campus and is composed of the following faculty members:

1. Dr. ROSS R. RICE, Chairman.

2. JOHN A. COCHRAN

3. RICHARD W. EFFLAND

4. JOHN P. DECKER

5. WALLACE ADAMS, Chairman of the Faculty Assembly.

-4-

Pages 173 and 174: The Phoenix FBI sought and received permission to send members of a faculty committee an anonymous letter slandering Starsky.

Dear Sir:

It seems appropriate that you should be informed of one of the most recent activities of Morris J. Starsky. Starsky learned of a suicide attempt by one of his close campus co-workers, David Murphy. Feeling that Murphy could no longer be trusted as a member of the campus socialist group, Starsky demanded that Murphy return all literature and other materials belonging to the socialist group. Murphy refused to give Starsky a quantity of socialist literature in his possession until Starsky would pay him a sum slightly in excess of $50 which was owed for telephone calls charged by Starsky to Murphy's telephone. Morris Starsky was indignant at Murphy's independent attitude and at 2:00 A. M. on April 5, 1970 he, accompanied by his wife Pamela and two young male associates, invaded Murphy's apartment and under threat demanded return of the socialist literature. When Murphy refused unless Starsky paid the phone bill, Starsky told him that his two associates would beat him unmercifully. Murphy, convalescing from a recent hospital stay, was under great fear of bodily harm or death and surrendered the literature.

I find this episode interesting. Where did Starsky learn of the effectiveness of smashing into a person's home at 2:00 A. M.? Also, of utilizing four persons to threaten the health or life of someone? Is this an example of academic socialism? Should the ASU student body enjoy the guidance of such an instructor? It seems to me that this type of activity is something that Himmler or Beria could accept with pride. If Starsky did not enjoy the prestige and sanctuary of his position he would be properly punished for such a totalitarian venture. Unfortunately, Murphy is too terrified to testify against Starsky. This is another example of Starsky's brand of academic socialism.

/s/ A concerned ASU alumnus

174

ROUTE IN ENVELOPE

SAC, Phoenix   (b) (7)

(b) (7)

Director   REC   (b) (7)

COINTELPRO - NEW LEFT

Reurairtel 4/5/70.

Authority is granted to make the anonymous mailing as suggested in referenced airtel. These letters may be sent to those recipients listed in that communication.

Prior to mailing, however, you should change the format in order to delete the caption "Anonymous Letter to Members of the Faculty Committee on Academic Freedom and Tenure, Arizona State University."

Closely follow this matter and keep the Bureau advised of results.

(b) (5)

Leaving little to chance, FBI headquarters directed Phoenix to "delete caption 'Anonymous Letter . . .'" before mailing.

175

Dear Senator:

I am indeed pleased to note that you are chairing a committee to investigate the activities of dissident elements on our college campuses. I trust that this effort will not become just another "study" but will actually result in concrete results to rid our universities and colleges of the disruptive activities of radicals, leftists and nihilists.

In this connection, I have taken upon myself a small project regarding the background of Professor David Herreshoff, of the English Department at Wayne State University.

It occurs to me that our college youth, who are going through a period of their lives during which they are most liberal and idealistic in their attitudes, are being exploited and subverted by certain faculty members in our colleges. Students by and large, experience these libertarian attitudes, graduate, then pass into the society and address themselves to their personal needs and objectives within the framework of our ongoing society. Very few of them become, and fewer yet, remain active in radical or disruptive activities such as campus take overs. However, it is these peculiar members of faculty who year in and year out use their positions to imbue the students with the philosophies and ideologies that provide a continuous stream of chaotic, militant incidents across the nation.

Why must the taxpayers of this state continually funnel their money into institutions which provide financial security and a ready made captive audience to professors who openly support through word and deed, avowed enemies of this country? Their heroes are the Che Guevaras, Maoists, Trotskyites, Stalinists and the anti-Christs. If they support any form of government at all it is at best socialistic or communistic.

Let these destroyers spew forth their ideas in public halls to those audiences who seek their words, but let us deny them speakers platforms in the classrooms of our educational institutions!

Prof. Herreshoff is active in political action and social groups existing on the campus at Wayne State University. However, it is rather enlightening to note which groups these are. He is the listed faculty sponsor for: the W.E.B. DuBois Club; Students for a Democratic Society; Student Mobilization Committee; and, the Young Socialist Alliance. I'm sure you recognize these "groups" as the very ones continually noted

Pages 176 and 177: Beginning and end of an eight-page phony letter supplying FBI-compiled information on Pro-

176

cooperation with the Selective Service System. A protest
march took place next to State Hall while the SDS group
met with vice-president James Mc Cormick. Prof. David
Herreshoff, English instructor, pointed out that the
American Civil Liberties Union is preparing to test the
constitutionality of various aspects of the draft, including
the ranking of students. "The University has taken the
position of cooperating with all public bodies", said
Herreshoff. "Our group pointed out that some public bodies
shouldn't be cooperated with."

An article by David Herreshoff appeared in the
May 6, 1968, issue of "The South End", Wayne State University
student publication, captioned, "the radical vs. liberal:
a view of social order".

An article appearing in the "Detroit News",
October 21, 1967, Final edition, captioned "Detroiters
Join D.C. Protesters" revealed that while Detroiters waited
to board buses outside MacKenzie Hallon the WSU campus
for the trip to Washington, D.C., to join the anti-war
protesters in a march on the Pentagon, a short rally was
held on the steps of State Hall, across Cass Avenue from
MacKenzie Hall. Article continues that several speakers,
including Dr. David Herreshoff, a Wayne English professor,
denounced the United States war effort in Vietnam. Dr.
Herreshoff, a frequent campus critic of United States policies,
said, "This is not just an American movement--we are part
of a world movement". He referred to the "genocidal burning
of the people of Vietnam by the people running our country".

On April 24, 1968, an open letter to the student
body was published in "The South End", which reads: "We,
the undersigned organizations and individuals, urge all
students who are against the war in Vietnam to vote on
Tuesday and Wednesday in the 'Choice '68' elections for
(1) an immediate withdrawal of American forces from Vietnam
and (2) a permanent cessation of the bombing of North
Vietnam." Among the signatures appeared Dr. David Herreshoff,
English Department...

I am preparing more information of this type
concerning Prof. Herreshoff and shall send it to you at
a later date.

Very truly yours,

A Fed-up Taxpayer!

*fessor David Herreshoff to encourage a witch-hunt by a
state senator investigating student dissent.*

Washington, D.C.
May 29, 1959 .

illian E. Manning
uperintendent
D.C. School System
415 12th Street, N.W.
Washington, D.C.

Dear Sir,

I am writing this letter directly to you as Superintendent
of the D.C. School System because of the severity of the accusations
which I am making against a teacher in the D.C. system. I am well
aware of your interest in the quality of education in this, the
Capitol city, and I am sure that you will take a responsible attitude
toward the information which I am furnishing.

As a resident of a large apartment building at 1801 16th
Street, N.W., I have become aware of the activities of another
resident. Miss Maude White, who is a teacher in the local elementary
school at 13th and S Streets, N.W. I have learned that since January
of this year, Miss White has held weekly meetings of a socialist youth
group which is active in the Washington area. From literature found
in our hallways, I have determined that this group is known as the
Young Socialist Alliance and from personal observation I have learned
that approximately twenty individuals attend these meetings each
Sunday evening at Miss White's apartment.

The literature belonging to this group advocates an overthrow
of our present system of government in a way similar to the Cuban
revolution of Fidel Castro. The printed policy of the group supports
violent activities against established authority, particularly the
police, and considers ghetto and student rioting as the beginning of
the violent revolution.

In a recent copy of their national magazine, The Young
Socialist, it is suggested that anyone interested in the organization
can contact Terrill Brubaok at 1801 16th Street, N.W., Apartment 610.
This is apparently the same individual who has been living with Miss
White for the last five months. I have noticed him on numerous
occasions parking Diamond Cab #280 in front of the apartment building.

*Pages 178 and 179: This anonymous FBI letter red-baiting
Maude White (Wilkinson) professed to be from "a concerned*

178

I bring this information to your attention in order to protect the D.C. School System from the menace of a teacher who does not have the interests of the children or the country at heart. I am certain that a responsible school administrator like yourself would not allow a revolutionist to indoctrinate the fertile minds of grade school children.

Since most of this information is actually public knowledge, only limited investigation by your office will be necessary to verify these accusations. For my own protection, I am not signing this letter. I assure you that this lack of identification in no way affects the veracity of the information contained herein.

I sincerely hope that your investigation and appropriate action can be completed before the start of the next semester. I am sure you will agree that the children and the country deserve to be protected.

A Concerned Citizen

citizen" worried that she would "indoctrinate the fertile minds of grade school children."

179

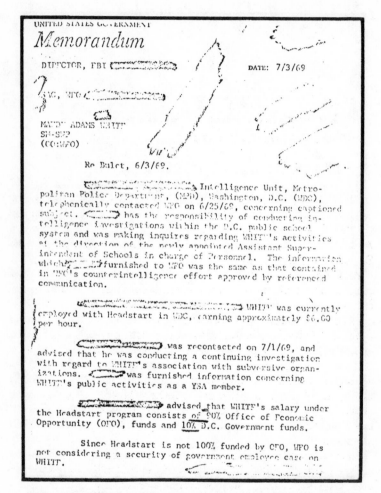

UNITED STATES GOVERNMENT

Memorandum

DIRECTOR, FBI ⟨̶̶̶̶̶̶̶⟩   DATE: 7/3/69

SAC, WFO ⟨̶̶̶̶̶̶̶⟩

MAYDE ADAMS WHITE
SM-SWP
(CO:WFO)

     Re Bulet, 6/3/69.

     ⟨̶̶̶̶̶̶̶̶̶̶̶̶̶̶̶̶̶⟩ Intelligence Unit, Metro-
politan Police Department, (MPD), Washington, D.C. (WDC),
telephonically contacted WFO on 6/25/69, concerning captioned
subject. ⟨̶̶̶̶⟩ has the responsibility of conducting intelligence investigations within the D.C. public school
system and was making inquires regarding WHITE's activities
at the direction of the newly appointed Assistant Superintendent of Schools in charge of Personnel. The information
which ⟨̶̶̶̶⟩ furnished to WFO was the same as that contained
in WFO's counterintelligence effort approved by referenced
communication.

     ⟨̶̶̶̶̶̶̶̶̶̶̶̶̶̶̶̶̶̶̶̶⟩ WHITE was currently
employed with Headstart in WDC, earning approximately $6.00
per hour.

     ⟨̶̶̶̶̶̶̶̶̶̶̶⟩ was recontacted on 7/1/69, and
advised that he was conducting a continuing investigation
with regard to WHITE's association with subversive organizations. ⟨̶̶̶̶⟩ was furnished information concerning
WHITE's public activities as a YSA member.

     ⟨̶̶̶̶̶̶̶̶̶̶̶̶̶⟩ advised that WHITE's salary under
the Headstart program consists of 90% Office of Economic
Opportunity (OEO), funds and 10% D.C. Government funds.

     Since Headstart is not 100% funded by OEO, WFO is
not considering a security of government employee case on
WHITE.

*This 1969 FBI memo documents the systematic collabora-
tion of the bureau, school administrators, and the local
police red squad to hunt down and purge leftist teachers.*

9 The fight to stop Cointelpro goes before the public

Peter Camejo and Syd Stapleton walked into NBC's Washington studios at 6:15 on the morning of March 19, 1975. At 7:00 a.m. the "Today" show went on the air. A few minutes later millions of Americans first learned of the FBI's conspiracy to destroy the Socialist Workers party.

Readers of the *New York Times* who had picked up that day's paper when it hit the street the night before were the first to find out about the story. The main headline was about the CIA's multi-million-dollar operation to retrieve a Soviet submarine off the floor of the Pacific. But also on the front page was an account of the FBI's Cointelpro plot against the socialists.

Peter Camejo is the SWP's presidential candidate. Syd Stapleton is national secretary of the Political Rights Defense Fund. After their appearance on the "Today" program, they drove to a news conference. There the PRDF released copies of the Cointelpro papers and individual FBI files on several SWP members.

Soon after the Washington news conference, reporters dispatched stories about the contents of the FBI files to newspapers and television and radio stations across the country. That evening and the next morning millions more learned about the FBI plot against their democratic rights.

In the following weeks the PRDF amassed some 600 newspaper clippings on this story. While this hardly compared to the deluge of publicity surrounding the Watergate scandal, it did represent an important breakthrough in alerting the American people to the systematic crimes of the federal spy agencies. The coverage in the major news media, reaching tens of millions of people, included the following:

• A March 19 Associated Press dispatch was carried in 170 daily papers in thirty-seven states. It was front-page news in 50 papers.

• The *New York Times* ran a detailed page-one story, plus a background article on the SWP. The *Times* story was picked up by at least twenty-five dailies.

• The AP sent out five separate follow-up articles.

• United Press International distributed two different stories.

• The *Washington Post* carried a page-one article.

• It's more difficult to measure the response on radio and television, although most Americans rely on them for news. The "Today" interview was the most significant.

"Every single major paper carried at least one story on the documents," said Cathy Perkus of the PRDF national staff. "The press treated the story very seriously. They saw the FBI behavior revealed in the documents as clearly illegal. I believe our assertion that these sorts of things are still going on after the FBI's alleged 1971 cut-off date for the program was accepted." The charge that Cointelpro continues—whatever it's now called—is central to the suit.

The front page of the March 20 *Houston Chronicle* carried a big headline about Dan Fein's FBI file. He had been the SWP's candidate for mayor in the previous election.

Newspapers in Minnesota, New Jersey, New York, and Wisconsin ran stories about illegal FBI activity in their areas.

The *Los Angeles Times* sent a staff writer to Arizona to report on what happened to Morris Starsky, the Cointelpro victim who was fired from his teaching position at Arizona State University. The reporter called FBI headquarters in Washington to ask why the FBI had launched this attack on Starsky and the SWP. The FBI refused to comment. But, interestingly, they did send him a copy of red-baiting remarks inserted into the *Congressional Record* by Representative Larry McDonald, a leading member of the John Birch Society.

A good many of the files involved attacks on the Black civil rights movement. Several North Carolina papers printed stories on an operation in that state. One of the AP stories, which concerned the North Carolina incident, was featured in papers throughout the South.

New York City's major Black paper, the *Amsterdam News,* ran a front-page story on FBI attempts to block collaboration between the NAACP and socialists. Syndicated Black political commentator Chuck Stone wrote about how the new interest in Marxism among some Blacks relates to the FBI assault on the SWP.

The *Guild Reporter,* put out by the Newspaper Guild, described how the "FBI misused the press."

The *Militant* has provided the most thorough coverage by far of the Cointelpro story—with several news articles and a twelve-part "Cointelpro Papers" series.

Others reporting the story included important papers in several different countries, campus papers, Liberation News Service, *Rights* magazine, and "alternative newspapers" in many cities.

Three months later, on June 24, the PRDF turned over to the news media a new group of files coughed up by the FBI. Again, it was big news.

The major national news sources—AP, UPI, the *New York Times,* the *Washington Post*—all featured stories. Syd Stapleton appeared on the network "CBS Morning News."

The release of the documents rated banner headlines in the *Houston Chronicle,* the *Cleveland Plain Dealer,* and the *Washington Star*—all papers in cities where FBI dirty work was uncovered.

Stories on other local Cointelpro plots unmasked by the files were featured in newspapers in St. Louis; Milwaukee; Atlanta; Detroit, Kalamazoo, and Muskegon, Michigan; Indianapolis; Portland; and Austin. Some of these stories were in turn reprinted in other cities.

Muhammad Speaks covered an Atlanta PRDF news conference where it was revealed that the FBI worked with the *Atlanta Constitution* to red-bait the YSA and the antiwar movement in that city in 1968. (The *Constitution* was the only paper to suggest the FBI files might be forgeries.)

Perhaps more revealing than the level of news coverage was the amount and character of editorial comment. The PRDF has received editorials on the first set of files alone from a total of thirty-six newspapers.

Several columnists commented in one way or another on the release of the Cointelpro papers. Included were nationally syndicated columnists Nicholas Von Hoffman, Mary McGrory, Tom Wicker, Arthur Hoppe, and Patrick Owens. James Wechsler, an editor of the *New York Post,* devoted two of his daily columns to the subject, and *Village Voice* columnist Nat Hentoff mentioned it.

Conservative political commentator James J. Kilpatrick chose the topic for remarks broadcast nationwide on the CBS radio network.

Taken together this media response presents an illuminating picture of the current controversy around the role of the FBI.

The first thing that stands out is that nowhere is there any attempt at all to defend the Cointelpro conspiracy. On the contrary, it comes in for scathing criticism: "To the list of organized crime operations, add the FBI. . . . thoroughly illegal"—*Dayton* (Ohio) *Daily News.* "Tactics ranging from the bizarre to the despicable"—*Des Moines* (Iowa) *Register.* "Frightening, chilling"—*Philadelphia Inquirer.* "Illegal and unconstitutional"—*Niagara Falls* (New York) *Gazette.* "Gutter tactics"—Ogdensburg, New York, *Advance-News.* "Gestapo tactics"—*St. Louis Post-Dispatch.* "It reads a lot like lies and libel . . . like a mixture of the late Joseph McCarthy and the worst of Watergate."—Bruce Morton, "CBS Morning News."

Kilpatrick's remarks over CBS radio must have articulated the feelings of many who share his political views: "I hope to remain a friend of the bureau, but the disclosure of the FBI's outrageous and contemptible harassment of the Socialist Workers party is enough to put a crimp in any friendship."

Many observers have noted the SWP's legality: "A legal American political party. . . . not accused of violating any laws"—*St. Paul Pioneer Press.* "Views never were shown to be subversive or in any way endangering freedom in our democracy"—*Blade,* Toledo, Ohio. "Perfectly lawful American political party, entitled to exist alongside the Republican party [and] the Democratic party"—Charleston, West Virginia, *Gazette-Mail.* "Legal political party"—*Minneapolis Star.*

Conspicuously absent for the most part is any tone of old-fashioned red-baiting. As the Scranton, Pennsylvania, *Times* saw it, their "sin in the eyes of J. Edgar Hoover [was] believing that a brand of socialism would be better economically and politically for the United States than the present system."

After making points like those, many observers went out of their way to insert some disparaging remark about the SWP. A couple of editorials described the SWP as minuscule. "The F.B.I.'s Appetite For Very Small Potatoes" was the headline on Nicholas Horrock's analysis in the Sunday *New York Times.*

On the one hand, these writers think the FBI is urgently in need of a face-lifting to recapture its authority, and this is their way of putting the FBI down for what they see as wasting time and money.

But it isn't very surprising that the SWP is described in this way. The party is small by most standards. Certainly, in terms of American political parties—where the capitalist Democratic and Republican parties monopolize the scene—the SWP seems irrelevant to most commentators. Some were no doubt genuinely confused about why the FBI paid so much attention to the SWP and YSA. It was a sign of J. Edgar Hoover's "paranoia," concluded a few.

J. Edgar Hoover, in any case, is not central to the issue. There is ample evidence that Cointelpro-type operations continue after his death. But for all his idiosyncracies, he was a devoted servant of the ruling class. His job was to run a political police force—one that was cloaked in secrecy—and he did just that for fifty years. It's dirty work.

Most people believe that in a democracy there is not really supposed to be a secret police. Cointelpro, as a matter of fact, was never meant to be known to the American people. That's why Hoover made a big display of canceling the program after it came to light in 1971.

The Cointelpro papers and the other files reveal some stupid FBI blunders and misestimates. The total picture, however, is of cool, calculating technicians, not crazed paranoids, going about the business of secretly combating people who are challenging the rule of the rich. That's the FBI's job.

The American ruling class is very farsighted. Although socialism is still relatively uninfluential in the political life of this country, that is not true on a world scale. The rulers realize this. They foresee a potential socialist challenge here. They study the history of past American radicalizations in which socialists have been prominent. They can also see—more clearly than many media commentators—that socialists have had some role in current social struggles.

In an interview with *Newsday,* Peter Camejo put it this way: "Hoover realized you can't judge a movement only by numbers. He realized that the party was a catalyst in the anti-war movement. Break us and you've broken the back of the anti-war movement, is the way he reasoned it."

All the big newspapers and television and radio networks are

[EDITORIAL, FRIDAY, OCTOBER 10, 1975]

Enough Is Enough

The official position of the Federal Bureau of Investigation and the Department of Justice on the bureau's counterintelligence program (Cointelpro) is that it was foolish, misguided and sometimes illegal and that it was ended in April, 1971. Yet, according to F.B.I. documents recently obtained by the Socialist Workers' party in a lawsuit against the bureau, some Cointelpro techniques were being employed at least as late as December, 1973.

The documents show that after April, 1971, the bureau continued to contact members of the Socialist Workers' party and its youth affiliate to inform them of the bureau's knowledge of their political activities and then to seek more information about those activities. The bureau also continued to contact members of the organization by telephone to gain personal information about them under the pretext of doing a jury duty survey. Such methods were used on at least 34 occasions after the program was supposedly ended.

The Socialist Workers' party is a legal American political organization. Although it has been the subject of wiretap surveillance for thirty years, no indictments and no convictions have been obtained by the Government. The only conceivable purpose of the continuation of the Cointelpro techniques is harassment and disruption of legitimate political activity.

Attorney General Levi has recently expressed his high regard for the F.B.I. and has characterized some recent criticism of the organization as unfounded. The criticism might fade more quickly if it were clear to the bureau that disruption of legitimate political activity is not part of its mandate and if it could be demonstrated to the American people that when the Government says it has terminated a course of improper conduct, it actually has done so.

owned by wealthy capitalists. They have an interest in how the dispute over the FBI and CIA is resolved. Commentary in the news media is a reflection of a discussion now going on in ruling circles.

There is wide agreement that both the FBI and CIA need a new coat of paint. That is the goal of the current investigations. The *New York Times* has urged "the slumbering F.B.I. oversight committees in Congress . . . to develop some clear new rules of conduct for the bureau."

Writing in the *Saturday Review,* former CIA official Tom Braden predicted, "Various committees now investigating the agency will doubtless find error. They will recommend change; they will reshuffle. But they will leave the monster intact."

At the same time the investigations carry a certain overhead. They can lead to uncovering new scandals that compound the problem of restoring credibility to the institutions. That's what is now happening with the new discoveries of CIA assassinations and FBI burglaries.

New FBI Director Clarence Kelley has already taken steps to improve the agency's image. He has given frequent news conferences and interviews, something Hoover shied away from. Local FBI offices, which have always refused to talk to the media, have been sending agents for special training in public relations.

The socialist suit raises more substantial questions than the FBI's image. It calls for a halt not only to Cointelpro-style harassment but to political surveillance. A short-lived victory was won in December 1974 when a federal judge banned FBI spying at the YSA's annual convention. The temporary ruling was later substantially weakened by Supreme Court Justice Thurgood Marshall.

"No responsible Government official now advocates a total ban on electronic surveillance," the *New York Times'*s Horrock wrote. That remains true.

None of the editorials came out and squarely condemned spying. A couple of papers explicitly endorsed it. The problem was that the FBI "went beyond keeping an eye on the group"— *Atlanta Journal.*

In an article on the Congressional investigations into the FBI, Horrock found that "the F.B.I. has been far less criticized for investigations leading to prosecutions than it was for its so-called 'counterintelligence program.'"

Attorney General Edward Levi offered a rather half-hearted criticism of Cointelpro. He labeled the operation "foolish because [it] doesn't work very well" and "outrageous because I think there's enough dishonesty and lack of candor and incivility in our society as it is."

FBI Director Kelley hasn't even gone that far. In fact, he openly defended Cointelpro at a news conference. It was meant "to do something that would ultimately . . . benefit the nation," he said.

A retired FBI official, former assistant director William A. Sullivan, was even more forthright in his endorsement of the conspiracy. On July 6, 1975, he appeared—with Kelley's blessings—on CBS-TV's "Face the Nation." A reporter asked about the anti-SWP Cointelpro. Sullivan was forced to admit that the SWP had done nothing illegal. "We have no evidence to this date that I know of that they've ever been involved in any violent activities," he said.

Then why is the FBI so interested in the SWP? "This group advocates the overthrow of the United States government by force and violence." That is patently false. The SWP has replied to that slanderous allegation in answers to government questions submitted to the court in conjunction with the suit.

Sullivan endorsed sending letters to employers to get SWP members fired. "The only mistake that I think that we make in an instance like that was sending an anonymous letter and not signing J. Edgar Hoover's name to it. I think we owe the American people this type of information."

In an earlier interview with the campus newspaper of the University of California at Los Angeles, Sullivan was asked if there is "any law that allows the FBI to expose Communists." He said he knew of none. But, he added, "there is not any that I know of that say that we should not do this either."

Sullivan also told the UCLA paper that "Communists" are not entitled to equal protection under the law and are not entitled under the First Amendment to have private political associations.

An indication of the government's likely defense for its assault on the SWP can be seen in Larry McDonald's red-baiting tirades in the *Congressional Record*. McDonald unsuccessfully tries to link the SWP with foreign terrorist groups. The Birchite claims his information comes from his own personal research, but it has all the earmarks of FBI intelligence.

What Has Been Accomplished

What are the gains of the suit to date? In the first place, there is no reason to think that the information on FBI and CIA illegal activity made public so far would have ever seen the light of day without the initiative of the suit. For example, CIA files released through the suit show the agency spied on the SWP since 1950, while the official Rockefeller commission report said CIA domestic surveillance began only in the late sixties.

These revelations have helped educate the American people about the antidemocratic way the employing class maintains its rule. The resulting public outrage has helped put the FBI and the CIA on the defensive. Exposure of their operations, and potential exposure, in the current political climate makes the dirty work of these agencies much harder.

The socialist legal action has pushed Cointelpro to the center of the debate around the FBI. Under this pressure top government officials today insist that Cointelpro is over and done with. They say J. Edgar Hoover ended it on April 28, 1971. The date is significant. April 6, 1971, was the day that news reports of a break-in at the FBI's office in Media, Pennsylvania, shattered the secrecy surrounding the operation.

All available evidence argues convincingly that Cointelpro-style disruption and harassment continue.

Even the FBI memos that ostensibly discontinued Cointelpro are unmistakably worded to allow the agency to engage in future disruption. (These files are reprinted in the introduction to this book.)

Evidence in the socialists' suit includes scores of post-1971 Cointelpro-style incidents. This evidence indicates that the FBI got socialists fired from their jobs and thrown out of their apartments, tried to disrupt their personal lives, and attempted to pressure them into being informers.

The purpose of the suit is to defend the democratic rights of socialists and all working people. Already the exposures of these illegal actions and the response have begun to do that.

There is more to the story than what the FBI has admitted thus far. Cointelpro itself, massive as it is, is only part of the FBI's secret war on the SWP and the YSA and on others trying to change society. There are indications that the FBI undertook disruption actions before 1956 when Cointelpro began. Even during its so-called Cointelpro years the agency engaged in similar actions outside of that program and instead called them "investigative activity" or "racial matter" or "subversive matter."

The Cointelpro papers are still rigidly censored. The FBI maintains a right to keep secret information that the agency says might blow the cover of informers or "investigative methods." Even the Congressional committees investigating the FBI have had difficulty getting access to agency material. As *Time* magazine has said, "It seems unlikely that courts will force agencies to release information that would compromise . . . FBI methods."

But the efforts of the Socialist Workers party, the Young Socialist Alliance, and others continue. We can expect further progress in the battle to get out the full story and to put a stop to the FBI's crimes.